The Housekeeper's Secret

The Housekeeper's Secret

a memoir

Sandra Schnakenburg

Published 2024
Printed in the United States of America
Print ISBN: 978-1-64742-760-3
E-ISBN: 978-1-64742-761-0
Library of Congress Control Number: 2024911744

For information, address:
She Writes Press
1569 Solano Ave #546
Berkeley, CA 94707

Interior Design by Andrea Reider

She Writes Press is a division of SparkPoint Studio, LLC.

Names and identifying characteristics have been changed to protect the privacy of certain individuals.

"Love recognizes no barriers.
It jumps hurdles, leaps fences, penetrates walls
to arrive at its destination full of hope."

DR. MAYA ANGELOU

In loving memory of

Lee Metoyer

Contents

Introduction

On a cool autumn morning in October 1994, Mom stood whipping eggs at the marble-topped island in the kitchen. I was thirty-two years old, married, and living in Australia. I'd moved out of my childhood home fifteen years earlier, but once a year I flew home to visit Mom and Lee. Even as Lee had become frailer, as she'd grown thinner and quieter, Mom had avoided talking about what we were both thinking. But that morning, she turned to me and said gently, "Sandy, why don't you spend some time with Lee today? She won't be with us much longer."

Lee *not with us*. A world without Lee in it? It was almost unthinkable.

Walking down the steps to the lower level of the house, I heard the raspy wheeze of Lee's breathing and the whispering hiss of the oxygen machine. I tiptoed down the hall like a teenager hoping not to get caught coming home after midnight. The wall outside Lee's bedroom was covered in cherished memories—framed photos documenting the nearly three decades she'd been with our family. Group shots near a concession stand at Wrigley Field. A Christmas photo of a joyful Lee dressed in her pristine white uniform, cradling her beloved *Mr. Cub* book. A picture of Lee propping me up when I was five and burdened by a full-length cast on my right leg. My First Communion photo with Lee and Mom on each side of me, this time with Lee the injured one, a stark white plaster cast running from her thigh to her foot.

Lee's door was wide open, and she sat upright in bed, smiling. A tube traveled out of the oxygen tank, then split in two, and snaked to the back of her head and around to the front where two little tubes rested just inside her nostrils.

"Sandy," she whispered, "come here and sit with me."

I settled beside her on the light blue comforter, careful not to jostle her fragile frame. A slender beam of light shone through the little window in the corner, and my eyes darted to the dresser mirror where Lee's most treasured photos were securely tucked in the space between the mirror and its frame. One photo of her beloved husband and another of their cherished little boy, both tragically taken from her in a devastating car wreck. She'd brought these precious mementos with her in 1965 when she first arrived to work for our family. Over the years, I must have studied the images hundreds of times, wishing I'd known the boy, wishing I could have played with him, wishing Lee had that husband to hold her hand. I thought, soon she'll be reunited with them, the two souls she holds dearer than life.

Lee gently removed the oxygen tube from her nose and rested her frail hand on mine.

"Can I ask you something?" she whispered.

"Of course. Anything."

"I never wrote that book I wanted to write. And now I'm running out of time."

Many times through the years, Lee had said, "Someday I'm going to write a book, and nobody will believe it," but she never said any more about it. And she never showed any interest in writing, never jotting so much as a draft of a short story, but oh, how she loved words. Her books, her crossword puzzles, her dictionary—they were some of her favorite things in the world.

Now Lee looked up at me with weary eyes. "Will you write the book for me?"

Me? Was she serious? I was an accountant. An accountant who didn't also happen to be a writer. And I knew almost nothing about her life. As I'd always understood it, she'd come to work for my family shortly after the tragic car crash and had been part of our lives ever since. What stories from her early years belonged in a book? Had she been a showgirl? A courtesan? A spy? Somewhere in a locker was there a folder of correspondence between her and Harry Truman?

I said, "You mean the book you've been threatening to write for most of my life?" We both laughed, then Lee turned to the side and launched into a rattling, gasping coughing fit. It broke my heart to see her struggling for air. If I could, I would have given her my breath.

She stopped coughing and dabbed delicately around her mouth with a tissue. "Well?"

Her request hung in the air.

For three decades, Lee had done everything I'd ever asked her to do and a thousand things I needed but hadn't asked for.

She untangled my necklaces and helped search for lost clothes. She tended to my viruses and cuts and sprains. She sewed patches on my jeans. She safeguarded my secrets. She nurtured my broken heart. And now, for the first time, she was asking me for something.

I stumbled over my reply. "I don't . . . I don't know if . . . It's just that I'm not . . ." Her eyelids grew heavy. "I don't even know what story you're talking about, Lee. We'd have to . . ."

"Will you try?" she whispered as her eyes closed.

"Yes," I answered, holding her delicate hand. "I'll try to do this for you."

Lee let out a sigh and drifted off to sleep.

I had no idea how I was going to write the story of a woman who'd sidestepped every personal question I'd ever asked her. Whenever I'd asked about her childhood, her family, her love life, her educational experiences, or anything else personal, she'd offered only a wisp of an answer, like, "Oh, that was a long time ago," then ended the conversation with, "Finish your homework."

I'd always thought it strange she revealed so little, but I assumed the deaths of her husband and child had been so painful she'd simply wanted to leave her past in the past. Now I vowed to find out as much as I could by spending the next several days by her side and this time going after information like an investigative reporter. I would finally learn the hidden truths about my beloved Lee. The more I thought about it, the more excited I became that she was finally ready to share them with me. If Lee wasn't going to be with us much longer, I'd have to start information gathering right away. And then I'd figure out how to turn it all into the most compelling book.

After I tiptoed back upstairs, Mom and I walked outside to the serene lake just across the road from her property and strolled along its banks, reminiscing about Lee and some of the countless wonderful memories we'd created together over the years. From the look of Mom's pinched forehead and the sound of her uneven breathing, I could tell she was struggling to accept what it would mean to go on without Lee in her life. I hurt for my mother who had developed a deep friendship with the woman who had come into her life as a housekeeper. Now the two of them were like an old happily married couple, remarkably compatible and sweetly dependent on each other.

Later that night, I retired to Mom's guest bedroom, a comforting space painted in soft pinks and purples. Matching drapes framed the windows, and a bouquet of freshly picked lilies from Mom's garden sat on the dresser. I snuggled in the warm blankets and thought about Lee downstairs, alone in the darkness of her room. I wondered if she was comfortable. I wondered if she felt sad to be leaving Mom. I wondered if she was afraid of death.

That night I thought of all the questions I'd soon ask her. I'd delicately inquire about her husband and son and would be more assertive as I dug into her early years, her family ties, her romances, and her work experience. What kind of girl had she been? Had she been close to her mother? What had she been like in school? How had she become such a passionate base-ball fan? What had she dreamed for her life, and now, how did she feel about the path she'd chosen? The questions sprawled across my mind like sparkling stars in the night sky.

This would be wonderful, I decided. I was going to spend the next several days and weeks by my beloved Lee's side, talking woman to woman, getting to know her intimately and giving her the thing she wanted most.

After a long, solid sleep I went downstairs, armed with a pen and notebook, ready to hear the first "nobody would believe it" stories from the life of my second mother. As I neared the kitchen, I saw my mother sitting at the table, her face buried in her hands.

When she heard me walk in, she looked up, her eyes red and flooded with tears. Then her lip quivered and she gasped, "She died last night."

It was November 2017, twenty-three years since I'd made my promise to Lee, and now my research had pointed me to Manteno, Illinois. I drove through Kankakee County, practically hypnotized by the repetition of fields and farms along the highway, and then arrived at the city limit. I looked up and saw a sign that read: MANTENO, POPULATION 9,300. Another sign just below it read: FOR MORE INFORMATION, CALL THE CHAMBER OF COMMERCE. That was it! *Exactly* what I needed. I pulled to the side of the road, jotted down the number, then kept driving toward the hospital.

Manteno felt like the riskiest part of this archaeological dig. It was the home of the mental hospital that held the answers to so many of my questions. I was headed there with no plan, just a burning sense that I had to walk its halls, feel its grass under my feet.

The hospital's entrance felt like the opening to an English country estate. Majestic oak trees provided shelter from radiant sunshine and cast shadows along the long, paved driveway. The hospital's black iron gate, winding asphalt driveway lined with black lanterns, and stately main building reminded me of my childhood home on Rainbow Road in Barrington, Illinois. The similarities were eerie.

The center section of the building commanded attention as it reached high above the surrounding buildings whose symmetrical wings seemed to reach out in hope of taking flight. As I continued deeper into the property, I came upon run-down cottages that seemed completely out of place relative to the institution's grand entrance. The cottage walls were covered in angry, chaotic graffiti. I took a deep breath. *What is this place?*

Moments later, I dialed the number from the Manteno Chamber of Commerce sign.

A gentle female voice answered, "Hello, may I help you?"

I cleared my throat. "Is there someone I can speak to who knows about the legends of Manteno State Hospital?"

"Oh yes, Dick Balgeman. He worked there for years. He knows everything about the hospital."

My heart started racing. "May I speak with him, please?"

"He's in a meeting, but I'll ask him to call you right back."

This was it. I was going to hear answers I hoped would tie up the last loose ends of the story of Lee's life. I'd already learned things that had astonished me, truths that had given me dark, fitful nightmares. But I needed to hear the rest.

I did get that call from Dick Balgeman, and the sound of his voice sent my heart thundering. This man was going to tell me about Manteno State Hospital's dark, devastating history. He knew how the place ran. He knew what went on in the hallways and behind the doors. Had he known *her*?

Part One

Summer

"There is always that one summer that changes you."

Beth Merlin

1

It's strange to me that while I vividly remember the day Lee came into my life, I have almost no awareness of my life before she was in it. It was as if her arrival created a flash so bright it washed out all prior memories. That said, I can't be sure whether my memory of her first day with us is my own or was planted in my mind by my mother, who recounted the event for many years afterward. Again and again, I'd plead, "Tell me about the day Lee came to stay." And every time I asked, Mom shared the details of that day as if she were reading it from a storybook, starting with the bright blue sky, the household in immaculate order, us kids bouncing with eager anticipation. Whether the memory was all mine or crafted by storytelling, not since that summer afternoon in June 1965 when I was three and a half have I met anyone so life-changing.

The sun was brilliant along the tops of the trees that lined our long driveway. Our new housekeeper was coming from Chicago to Barrington, our village of giant lawns and tall trees, roughly forty miles northwest of the Loop, and most of my family was fidgety with anticipation. On that day, Mom wore a pink-and-yellow floral dress with matching yellow heels. Her hair was done up in a stylish beehive, and she smelled good. Our whole house smelled good. Mom had gotten up early to make homemade rolls, and she'd asked me to butter the pan, then rewarded me with bits of the raw, chewy dough. I opened my mouth as wide as a baby bird to receive those little pieces of yumminess. Everything about the buzz in our house that morning said this new lady must be special.

As the rolls baked, I followed Mom into her bedroom where my sisters and I lined up and knelt beside her velvet bedspread to pray. Mom often asked us to pray with her when she needed help with a decision or when she was nervous about how something was going to turn out. I knew today's prayer was about our new housekeeper. I squeezed my eyes closed and pressed my hands together. *Lord,* I said in the silence of my heart, *please let the new housekeeper be a nice lady. Please let her be kind and not spank us or lock us in our rooms like the others. Please let her help my mom so Dad won't be so mean to her all the time. And please, pretty please, Lord, let her allow us to have candy.*

Sometimes in Mom's big bedroom, we'd pray for so long our knees would end up looking like dented pink patches of gravel. Other times, Mom sat on the edge of our beds and said our prayers with us before she tucked us in. She told me if we asked God for things that were important to us, he'd answer our prayers. I often wondered what my mom was asking God for during all that praying. I couldn't imagine what because it seemed to me adults could do and have anything they wanted. Adults could buy whatever they wanted and go to bed whenever they wanted. But there must have been things she still wanted because she spent a lot of time praying.

I never saw Dad pray at home, only in church. Every Sunday, we squished into his Cadillac, and he drove there fast because we were always running late. He squealed the car into the parking lot, then we all shuffled into the church and slipped into the front pew, which was usually empty. It was as if the congregation knew we'd show up late. After Dad prayed, his silence and his peaceful face made him seem nicer, but as soon as Mass was over and we were back in the car, he'd go back to being his cranky self.

Dad had a lot of stuff, a lot of kids and cars and houses and boats, but none of it ever seemed to make him happy the way a new thing made me happy, like the time I got a red Schwinn bike for Christmas. For Dad, none of that happiness ever showed up. He'd say, "I'm going to buy that property someday." "Someday I'll buy that golf course." "I'll own that boat someday." It was always big stuff, never simple, little things. Then, right after he bought this or that, he started talking about the next thing and the next thing. And it seemed that every day, morning until night, he was grouchy and grumbling about how much he needed to work so he could keep buying things.

I continued to kneel next to Mom as she prayed. I'd already run out of things to pray about, so I just stayed quiet, occasionally glancing at her, hoping she'd release me. Her eyes stayed closed, so I stood up and crept to the bedroom window to watch for the new lady. Soon afterward, I saw a yellow taxi gliding up the driveway.

"Here she comes!" I squealed, jumping up and down. I dashed out of the master bedroom to the top of our big staircase, which extended over a waterfall that cascaded into a pond stocked with koi fish. A huge glass window reached from floor to ceiling, and through the trees I could see the taxi getting closer. Mom hustled to the kitchen to remove the rolls from the oven.

The taxi rolled past a row of black lanterns, past giant wavy willow trees that stood next to the pond full of wild geese and ducks, past all the pink, purple, red, and yellow flowers my sisters and I had planted with Mom that spring. I pressed my forehead against the cold windowpane again, not wanting to take my eyes off the approaching car. The smell of the warm rolls blended with the sweet smell of freshly picked lilacs. Summer was finally here, and our new housekeeper was arriving. Life was perfect.

My four older sisters swarmed by the window for a better look as the taxi disappeared behind the bushes that hid our big house from the road.

"Ouch!" I cried. "Stop pushing!"

Outside, our St. Bernard, Pudgy, bellowed and then ran off yapping and nipping at the taxi's tires as the car approached the carport. At the sight of our new housekeeper sitting in the back seat, my stomach swirled around like a washing machine. What if Pudgy—our only rowdy dog out of six—ruined everything?

Dad said we always had to have six dogs to protect our family. Kim was a sweet German shepherd who did everything Dad asked her to do. Dana, the giant Great Dane, looked scary, but he was gentle as a kitten. Snoopy, a German shorthaired pointer Dad had gotten to help him hunt, loved to run around, but he obeyed commands to stop, sit, and lie down. Caesar was my Old English sheepdog, a lovable, hairy, playful dog that walked my sisters to the bus stop every day. Pee Wee was a yapping Chihuahua and the only dog allowed inside the house to cuddle because he was the only one Mom trusted not to drag in dirt and break valuable statues and other decorations. As I peered out the window and clenched the banister, I saw Pudgy was now bounding across the yard toward a squirrel. I breathed out with relief.

The taxi stopped under the carport.

"Mind your manners, children," Mom warned. "We don't want to scare her off before she gets to the front door."

My nine-year-old sister, Debbie, waved her hands and commanded, "Everyone line up on the stairs. She's coming inside any minute!" I stayed by the foyer window and waited. Finally, the driver got out of the taxi. He was a short man who wore a Cubs baseball cap and a tattered blue T-shirt. He opened the back door, and there the new lady sat very still. She had short, wavy hair and wore thick-rimmed, cat-wing glasses, light brown pants, and a gray coat. She just sat there. Why didn't she want to rush out and meet us? Why didn't she jump out of the taxi, singing, "*The hills are alive with the sound of music*"?

Mom lined up my sisters and me at the foot of the staircase, tallest to shortest, oldest to youngest, just like the von Trapp children, and barked instructions.

"Fix your hair."

"Hands to your sides."

"Stand still, be quiet."

We tried, but we couldn't stay still. Roseann, my oldest sister, at twelve and a half, rushed back to the window to see if the new lady had gotten out of the taxi, and we all followed like a line of marching penguins. With our faces plastered against the foyer window, we watched as the lady stretched one leg out of the back seat, then the other, and slowly stood. She moved with a shuffle, one foot pointed outward while the other dragged a little and pointed outward in the other direction. She reminded me of a duck, like a bent-over duck. Her wavy, short black hair looked shiny and wet. As she made her way to the front door, she kept a tight grip on her large black purse. I thought maybe her purse was too heavy. Maybe that's why she was bent over like that.

She stood patiently as the taxi driver pulled a little suitcase from the trunk. Then she looked up and saw our faces at the window. Her eyes sparkled as she flashed a warm smile.

Debbie hustled us from the window back to our positions at the bottom of the staircase next to the front door. Mom held baby Robert with both arms, so she had to step right up close to the door to be able to reach the handle. She opened the door wide before the lady even had a chance to knock.

"Welcome, Ms. Metoyer, please come in," Mom said in a soft, friendly tone.

The taxi driver stood behind the new lady and set her suitcase inside the front door, then he turned to leave.

The lady stepped forward and said, "Hello, my name is Lee Metoyer, but you may call me Lee." Her voice was gentle and soft.

"Lovely to meet you. I'm Mrs. Lillian Krilich, and you may call me Lillian. Welcome to our home."

"Glad to be here."

"May the children also call you Lee?"

"They may."

"Please allow me to introduce them. We've all been looking forward to your arrival."

My sisters each took a step forward, and I tried to wedge my way between them, hoping to catch the new lady's attention.

"Move it, Pee Wee!" Robin, my six-year-old sister, snapped. "You're in my way."

"Stop pushing everyone!" Barb squealed at Robin. At five years old, Barb was known for following rules.

Mom shot us an annoyed glance. Then she opened her arms wide toward Lee as if presenting a star on the stage. "Children, I'd like you to meet Lee, who will be our new housekeeper."

To Lee, she said, "Here we have my oldest daughter, Rose-ann. Then Debbie, Robin, Barb, and Sandy."

Lee said, "You're all such beautiful girls. It's so nice to meet all of you."

She said, "all." That meant she was including me! I didn't think I was pretty like my sisters because my thick, curly hair was always out of control, but Mom said it was nice hair and that I got it from her, and that always made me feel at least a little pretty.

Lee smiled at my baby brother in Mom's arms.

"And here is the newest addition, Rob."

"Oh my. You have a beautiful fam . . ." Lee struggled to get the words out and took a small step back. Sweat made her forehead shiny.

Mom spoke quickly, "It must have been an ordeal to get here. May I offer you a glass of cold water?"

Lee pulled a hanky from a pocket to wipe her forehead, and a piece of paper slipped out of her pocket and fluttered to the ground.

Mom bent over to pick it up. "Let me get that for you. Oh, it's the Prayer of St. Jude," she said, handing it back to Lee. "You must be Catholic too. St. Jude is one of my favorite saints."

"Mine too. Thank you, ma'am."

"Follow me. I'll get you a glass of water and then show you around the house."

"Yes, ma'am."

Mom led, Lee followed, and the rest of us trailed behind. Mom walked us all past the koi pond and into the family room where the walls behind the enormous bar area were covered with pictures of racehorses. Above a shiny black card table were two large paintings of clowns. The whole room kind of felt like Dad's. He spent a lot of time in there, and he chose the decorations. Then we all walked through the French doors that led to the kitchen.

Lee set her big Mary Poppins bag down. It was a pretty bag, black with a big handle, and I wondered if it held any magical objects. Because she was no longer holding the bag, I thought maybe her back would straighten from being so hunched over, but it didn't. Mom handed her a glass of water, and she drank it in one long swallow, then wiped her face with the napkin. She seemed nervous, but I couldn't imagine what she had to be nervous about. We all liked her. Lee let out a loud sigh, and her shoulders seemed to relax.

Mom fussed over Rob. "He's the boy we've been waiting for after having five daughters. My husband always wanted a son to be his namesake and follow in his footsteps."

Lee studied Robert for several seconds and smiled. Then she took a sweeping look at the kitchen. "Oh my, how wonderful," she gushed.

Our kitchen was pretty big. It had two big ovens, big enough to fit a giant turkey in each, and a microwave oven, which Mom said was one of the first ever used in a home. We called our microwave "a radar range," and the coolest thing about it was it heated leftovers in seconds, made a cupcake in one minute, and thawed frozen food really fast. It made me feel like we lived in George Jetson's house.

"I've never seen a kitchen table like that before," Lee said.

Mom ran her hand over the big peach-colored table where we ate most of our meals. "Yes, kidney-shaped tables are uncommon. We had this one custom-made. My husband thinks he has a knack for interior design, and I don't dare challenge his decisions. It's not worth the arguing."

Lee smiled and looked down at Rob again.

"Do you want to hold him?" Mom asked.

"Oh, yes."

Mom placed my baby brother in Lee's arms, and right away he made cute baby sounds and wiggled his arms all around. Mom smiled. "How sweet. Already he likes you."

"I love babies, and this baby boy is absolutely beautiful."

I hoped Lee could love me too.

Mom continued the house tour, and Lee gasped at the black-and-white zebra skin that hung on our foyer wall. *Oh no,* I thought. *I hope she doesn't think my dad killed the zebra. I'll bet she won't stay if she thinks Dad is a killer.*

As we stepped into the living room, we kids took our shoes off. We all knew to remove our shoes before entering the living room or dining room. But Mom didn't take her shoes off or ask Lee to take off hers.

Lee's eyes widened when she saw the bright lime-green carpet. "Oh my. Green must be your husband's favorite color."

Mom nodded, then led Lee through a glass door to the backyard patio, which was covered with indoor/outdoor red striped carpeting. Beyond the patio was our great big built-in swimming pool, and the pool water sparkled like glitter.

"Do you swim?" Mom asked.

"Oh, no, ma'am, I never learned."

I frowned. I was hoping she could teach me someday. All my big sisters knew how to swim, but I wasn't allowed beyond the steps on the shallow side.

Lee looked kind of tired, and my mom asked, "May I take Rob off your hands?" Lee handed the baby back to Mom.

Lee said, "That's quite a pool. I haven't seen anything like it." Then she squinted at the water. "Mrs. Krilich, may I ask what those yellow colors are at the bottom of the pool?"

"That's Tweety Bird—from the *Looney Tunes* cartoons. It was the children's idea."

"That's something else."

"Let's go back inside," said Mom, and she turned back to the house. I followed, but by then my siblings had grown bored and were splitting off in other directions.

In the kitchen, Lee asked, "Mrs. Krilich, do you mind if I have a cigarette?"

"Please feel free to smoke. My only request is that you don't smoke in bed. I've read stories about people falling asleep and burning down the house."

"I promise I won't smoke in bed, Mrs. Krilich."

Lee sat in a kitchen chair and reached inside her purse for a cigarette, which she placed between her lips and lit. As she puffed in and out, she looked out across the backyard. Her face looked peaceful when she smoked. As Lee rested in the kitchen chair inhaling and exhaling, Mom bounced Rob on her lap and kept talking about the house, the horse pasture, the apple orchard, the lake, the playground, the helipad, the tennis court. She talked about the horses and dogs and chickens and rabbits. Lee was so quiet, I was afraid she didn't like animals or the pool or the backyard or the kitchen. Usually, people oohed and aahed during a tour of our house.

Eventually, Lee exhaled a long gust of smoke. "Excuse me, Mrs. Krilich, are you expecting me to help with the animals and with the outdoors too?"

"Oh no, Lee, we have a caretaker who handles everything outside. And the children will help feed all the animals."

Robin and Barb ran into the kitchen. "Mom, when's dinner? I'm hungry," Robin said.

Mom jumped up. "Oh my, with all this excitement I forgot to start dinner. Lee, why don't I quickly show you your room downstairs before I put dinner on?"

Mom picked up Rob and held him in one arm as she waved Lee toward the basement staircase. I followed. Lee stopped on the last step, then looked back and up, smiling at us with a twinkle in her eyes.

As Lee entered the basement and looked around, her mouth dropped open. The space was huge and probably seemed even bigger because of its bright yellow walls and the enormous living room area that was decorated with a big blue three-seater couch, a coffee table, and a large Zenith television. The top of the television was big enough to use as a table for magazines and an ashtray.

"What's that over there in the corner?" Lee asked, looking across the room at a chalkboard that peeked out from a room about the size of a bathroom.

"That's a mini-playroom where the kids play school," Mom said.

"I love playing school!" I said, jumping up and down.

"Where does that door lead?" Lee asked, pointing across the room in the other direction.

"Inside that door is a shelter," my mother said. "During tornado warnings, we come down here for our safety from the storm until the warning is lifted."

I wondered if Lee had ever been in a tornado. We called the tornado room "the boiler room," and it seemed that all the important things that ran the house, like water, lights, and gas, went through that room somehow. The room was so big fifteen people could stand inside it at once, more if they were little. The boiler room was always warm, and whenever I was in it, I wanted out. It was creepy, and I was always afraid that someday I might get locked in there.

Mom walked past the blue couch and opened a set of wooden closet doors. "Here's our washer and dryer," she said.

"What's that over there?" Lee pointed to a white machine.

"That is our mangler iron to press bedsheets after washing and drying them."

"A mangler? I've never heard of that."

"I'll show you. If you like ironing, you might like the mangler, but you must be careful not to get your hands caught in it. Over here in this area, we also have an ironing station." Mom walked over to the other side of the room where an ironing board was set up next to a big refrigerator, also bright yellow. Next to that were a kitchen sink and cabinets.

"I may never leave the basement," Lee said with a chuckle.

"My husband thought of everything when he built the house. There are laundry chutes upstairs, so everyone in the family throws their dirty clothes into these magical cubbies, after which they go zipping down to the basement like on a giant playground slide."

Lee's face lit up like someone who'd just been told there was a roller coaster in the backyard.

Mom went on. "The door to the chute is right over there," she said, pointing to a closet door near the couch. "Let's show you your room and private area." Mom walked to the far end of the room to a set of wooden doors that opened like an accordion. "Here's your room. My husband sectioned this area for you," she said, sliding open a wooden partition as if she were unveiling a grand prize.

Lee stepped into the room and peered around in awe. In her room was a tall, extra-long single bed with a light blue bedspread. Next to the bed stood a large white dresser with a mirror attached. The floor of her room was covered in the same short, beige carpet that ran throughout the basement. Along the far wall was a full-size closet full of empty hangers and a table that matched her dresser.

"This is lovely, ma'am, I am so grateful," Lee said.

My mother smiled, and I could tell we were both feeling hopeful that this nice Lee might want to move in and give Mom the help she needed so much. "Finally, your shower, changing room, and bathroom are over here," Mom said. "I do apologize that your bathroom has only a shower, no bathtub."

Lee stood just inside the bathroom door and slid her hands in her pockets. Her eyes were wet with tears, and she let out an audible sigh. It was as if Mom had just told her she'd no longer have to sleep outside and be eaten by mosquitoes.

"What is it?" Mom asked.

"I'm incredibly grateful to have a shower stall rather than a bathtub. I forgot to mention to the agency that I do not take baths. Ever."

Mom tilted her head. She seemed to be thinking what I was thinking. Why would anyone hate baths? All the bubbles and the pretty smells, and then you get out and someone dries you with a big, warm towel and then you get into warm pajamas that smell like yummy laundry detergent.

Mom turned to lead us back up to the kitchen. "Why don't we all go upstairs and have a little snack now, then Lee can get settled in her room while I prepare dinner. Lee, would you like some coffee?"

"Oh, yes please, ma'am. I take my coffee black."

We followed Mom into the kitchen, where she placed Rob gently in the bassinet in the kitchen and prepared a plate of sesame seed crackers with cheddar cheese. Then she set an empty coffee cup in front of Lee.

Lee sat quietly, watching Mom set the plate on the table. Then she said, "I don't mean to be ungrateful, but I can't have sesame seeds. They get caught in my dentures."

Mom gasped, "You're far too young to have false teeth!"

"Oh, I know," Lee answered quickly. "But I didn't take care of my teeth. If I'd only listened to my parents and brushed every day . . ."

"Well, perhaps you can teach the children a thing or two about dental hygiene," Mom said.

Lee smiled shyly. "Yes, ma'am." She sipped her coffee, then lit another cigarette, which she sucked hard before tipping her head back and blowing smoke toward the ceiling in a gray stream. Robin, Barb, and I stood shoulder to shoulder watching her, and she beckoned us with her index finger. We skipped over to her, and she reached into her black leather bag and pulled out three Cracker Jack bagged surprises, each a different color, each with prizes inside. She placed them in her hands and made fists so we couldn't see what she was holding. "I have a little surprise for each of you," she said in a quiet, sing-songy voice, then stretched out her closed fists. "Well, come now, don't be shy, I don't bite. Pick one."

We looked at her, then at Mom.

"Go ahead, children, pick one," Mom said.

Robin looked at me. "Go ahead, Pee Wee. You go first."

I selected the orange bag and opened it. Inside was a ring, bright orange, my favorite color, with a picture of a castle on it. I slipped it on my finger, but it was way too big. Lee said, "Let me see it." I handed it to her, and she adjusted it. It fit perfectly after that, and I smiled as I admired the new ring on my out-stretched hand. Then I stepped closer to hug her. Lee wrapped me in a big bear hug, and I didn't want to let go.

Mom smiled at me. "Let me see what you have there." I extended my hand, and Mom said, "Oh my, what a special gift."

Barb opened a yellow charm necklace, and Robin's prize was a whistle.

"*Thank* you," Robin, Barb, and I said, almost in unison.

Clutching our prizes, my sisters and I glanced at each other and smiled. We all wanted Lee to stay.

$$\text{\textcurrency\textcurrency\textcurrency} 2$$

As I lay in bed on the night of Lee's arrival, I ran my fingers over the intricate details of my castle ring. Lee's gift comforted me. It was my favorite color and made me feel like a princess. With a whisper, I wished into the ring that Lee would stay with us forever. Then I thought hard about what I could do to help make that happen and tried to remember everything I could about the instructions Mom had given us a week earlier.

Mom had gathered us kids on the half-moon-shaped maroon sofa in the family room. Above us, mounted high above our massive stone fireplace, was a swordfish as long as a diving board. Its unblinking black eyes always sent a shudder through my body. It looked angry, and its anger always seemed focused on me. I sat on the end of the couch, next to a green-and-cream marble horse statue that stood about as tall as a table lamp. My sisters were lined up next to me, all of us sitting quietly at attention.

Our mother looked as if she was about to leave for a garden party, her pretty hair pinned up and her nails perfectly painted and shiny. She stood in front of us like a teacher addressing a classroom of new students. "Our new housekeeper arrives on Monday, and we want to make her feel right at home. Mind your manners as you do when your father is here. That means always offering to help her, no complaining, and no crying. We don't want her to leave because we have bad manners, do we?"

My sister Robin always had questions, and they always had a negative spin. "How do we know she's not going to spank us and lock us in our rooms like the other housekeepers did?"

"There will be none of that!" my mother said. "The agency says this new lady is very sweet. But there's one thing they asked of us—we're not to ask our new housekeeper anything about her family."

"Why not?" Barb asked.

"I'm told she lost her husband and son in a terrible car accident. That's very, very sad, and we can understand how it's something she wouldn't want to think about again, right?"

We all murmured in agreement.

Mom continued, "Mrs. Metoyer spent a lot of time in the hospital recovering from the shock of losing them, and the agency warned that if we press her to talk about them, she could end up back in a hospital."

When our dog, Silver, died a few months earlier, I'd cried for three days. I didn't understand what death meant; I thought Silver would be back. But even though I didn't yet understand the finality of death, I knew that having your husband and son die was probably worse than losing your dog.

Robin spoke up again. "But won't she want to remember them on their birthdays?"

"I'm sure she'll think of them on all their special days, but she may want to keep it private. We will respect her wishes," Mom said.

"Maybe we can be her new family!" I said.

"Yes, I hope so. Let's just make her feel good about being here."

That night before bed, Mom said, "Now let's pray." We knelt next to Mom and Dad's bed, all of us in a row, oldest to youngest.

Mom said, "Tonight, we're going to pray that our new housekeeper will be happy here and will want to stay with our family. We'll say a rosary for our intentions." She held out a basket. "Each of you pick one of these rosaries."

I asked, "Which beads on my rosary are for the Our Father?"

Mom was a devout Catholic, and she never minded explaining religious traditions and rituals. "Let's start from the top," she said. "We'll do the prayers before the rosary and state our intentions, which means we'll ask for God's help for specific things, like our new housekeeper coming tomorrow. Then we'll say a Hail Mary for faith, hope, and love on the first three beads, and then we'll begin the first decade, which is one Our Father and ten Hail Marys. There are five decades, meaning we do the same prayers five times. Just follow my lead and remember to rub the rosary with your fingers every time we say a prayer."

I did as I was told, and after each Our Father and Hail Mary I grew more and more tired, as always. The rhythmic chanting always lulled me into a kind of foggy-headedness, and soon my eyelids were so heavy I just sank to the floor asleep while everyone else continued to pray. That's how I ended the night of prayers about the new housekeeper, and when I woke up later in my bed, I hoped my failure to finish the prayers hadn't jinxed the whole thing.

The morning after Lee's first night with us, I jumped out of bed, brushed my teeth, changed my clothes, and ran downstairs. While the rest of the household slept, I waited outside the basement door until, finally, I heard her footsteps coming up from the basement. She opened the creaking door to the kitchen looking like a doctor's office nurse in an all-white uniform, complete with nylons and rubbery white shoes. Her jet-black hair was combed back in sleek waves and glistened with shiny hair products. From behind her bottle-thick glasses, her eyes met mine, and she smiled warmly at me.

"Good morning, Sandy, what are you doing up so early?"

She remembered my name! How did she remember my name? She'd only just met all of us last night. I shrugged my shoulders and said, "I don't know."

"Well then, why don't you help me make the coffee?"

The coffee! Coffee was a very adult thing—I knew that. No one had ever asked me to help with coffee.

Lee asked, "Can you tell me where the coffee pot is?"

"Over there." I pointed to the far end of the kitchen.

Lee held my hand and walked me to the tall, shiny coffee pot. She opened a cupboard just above it and pulled down a canister of ground-up coffee.

"Okay, now scoop out enough coffee to fill this filter. Let's count together. One, two, three, and four. Good girl. Now I'm going to fill the pot with water, and then you can push down the lid and push the red button to turn it on."

I looked down at Lee's white shoes as she shuffled to the sink to fill the pot with fresh water. What a funny walk she had,

kind of like her legs weren't put on quite right. Then she shuffled back to the coffee pot and pressed the lid down firmly.

"Okay, now you can push the red button." She lifted me so
I could reach it. What a great morning, I thought. Just Lee and
me.

While we waited for the coffee to finish bubbling and hissing, Lee opened the dishwasher.

"Can I help?" I asked her.

"Sure, you can. Can you show me where things go?"

"I can! The dirty dishes go on the left side of the sink, and
the clean dishes go over there," I said, pointing to the drying
rack. Then I pointed in all directions as I rattled off as many
kitchen facts as I could think of. "We keep cereals over there,
and that's where the bread goes. Mom keeps her baking pans
there, but the soup and spaghetti kinds of pots—those go up
there. Spices are in that drawer, but not the ones Mom uses
most, like salt and pepper—those go over here."

After I ran out of things to point out, Lee said, "Thank you
so much, Sandy. That was very helpful to me. I feel much more
comfortable in your kitchen now."

My heart swelled. I'd made a grown-up feel more
comfortable.

Shortly afterward, Mom joined us in the kitchen. Lee and
I had already set the kitchen table for breakfast, and the coffee
had just stopped bubbling and hissing.

"Good morning, Mrs. Krilich, may I get you a cup of coffee
that Sandy helped make?"

Mom raised her eyebrows and smiled. "Yes, thank you." I
was used to Mom dashing around the kitchen before meals,
but this morning, she sat at the table and sipped peacefully

while Lee opened and closed all the cupboards. After several minutes, Mom stood and said, "Okay, I'll get breakfast started."

And so it began. From then on, Mom and Lee began many of their days discussing what we kids had on our schedules—homework, birthday parties, sports, and chores like taking out the trash and feeding the dogs. Then they planned the next few meals and wrote the grocery list. Right away, I thought Mom seemed happier. She snapped less when my sister Debbie came home after curfew or if Barb was late to feed the dogs. And during Lee's first week, Dad was out of town, which always made the house a nicer place to be.

Lee couldn't drive—she didn't even have a license—but that wasn't a problem because Mom never liked leaving anyone else in charge of our safety on the roads. Lee seldom left the property when she stayed with us and was always home to meet us after school, even if Mom wasn't. And Mom and Lee seemed to balance each other perfectly in all the ways needed to run a household. Lee didn't know how to cook and preferred doing the dishes; Mom loved cooking and was good at it. Lee preferred not to handle other people's dirty laundry, opting instead to iron clothes and wrangle bedsheets. Mom preferred to be in charge of laundry to prevent delicate clothes from being damaged, and she had no interest in ironing.

One night after Lee had been with us for a little over a week, Dad returned from a business trip. I knew he was home because the next morning in the kitchen Mom was wearing a long, flowing dress, her hair elegantly tied up and pinned, and her makeup made her look as if she'd gotten ready for a fancy party. But she didn't seem as happy and calm as she'd been since Lee's arrival.

"Lee," she said in a tone that sounded as if her throat was tight, "my husband came home last night, and he'll be down for breakfast soon. I want you to know he isn't a morning person. If he starts yelling, please don't take it personally."

Lee's eyebrows shot up. "Yes, ma'am." She hustled over to the percolator to pour coffee. Then she rushed back to the dishwasher to finish emptying it of the previous night's dishes. Mom's lips looked tight, and she seemed to be concentrating harder than usual.

I couldn't remember a morning when Dad didn't yell at our mother. Just before he went away a week earlier, he'd made his typical kind of scene.

"I want *all* my shoes shined, every week!" he'd yelled.

"Bob, I can only do so much. When the new housekeeper arrives, things will go more smoothly," she said.

"Until then, I guess you'd better get off your lazy ass."

I hated the way he talked to her, but I wasn't going to get in the middle. Now as we waited for Dad to come downstairs for breakfast, Mom was all jitters, trying to make the morning scene perfect. "Lee," she said in a voice slightly higher than her usual, "can you please pour one glass of every type of juice we have in the refrigerator and set them in a row in front of Mr. Krilich's plate?"

Lee stood in front of the opened refrigerator. "But Mrs. Krilich, there are *seven* different types of juices in here."

"Yes, I know. Please pour them all. I'm hoping one of them will be the juice he wants today."

I could see Lee roll her eyes.

Mom laid a couple of newspapers on the table. "Every morning, place the *Chicago Sun-Times* and the *Chicago Tribune* in front of his place setting just so," my mother said, stacking one on top of the other, then sliding the top newspaper down a bit, then up a little, then back down. "He likes to be able to see the headlines on both papers."

"Yes, ma'am."

Just then I could hear Dad's heavy footsteps coming down the stairs. *Thump. Thump. Thump.* Like a fairy-tale giant. As he reached the bottom step, Mom cracked eggs into the sizzling pan faster than I'd ever seen her do.

"Lee, can you please pour Mr. Krilich a cup of coffee?"

"Yes, ma'am."

As Lee poured coffee into a cup, Dad strode through the French doors into the kitchen, and as always, he seemed to fill the room. His ocean-blue eyes gleamed, and his jet-black hair was styled like Elvis's except maybe a little more businesslike. His clothes always looked like they'd never been stained, and his nails were clean and smooth at the edges. He wore a bright purple shirt with a paisley tie, and the only thing that made him not look like a movie star was his belly. With a swift motion, he pulled back his chair, and it screeched as it scraped across the floor. Then he settled himself at the head of the table with a thump.

"Bob, I'd like you to meet Lee, she's our new housekeeper," Mom said.

Lee approached him slowly.

"Good morning, Mr. Krilich. My name is Lee, and it's a pleasure to meet you. I've been here for about a week helping Mrs. Krilich. May I pour you some coffee?"

"Yes, please." He glanced at her, then back to his newspapers, but he kept talking as he looked away. "It seems you've already lasted longer than most of your predecessors." He raised his cup to his lips, then took a sip before gently placing it back on the table. It was then I saw his face change, and I sat up straight and looked down at my plate. I knew this change. His face always scrunched like that right after he started to drink coffee and before he got cranky. I peeked up from my breakfast and saw Dad's eyes flash toward Mom, who was tending to business on the stove, preparing his eggs and buttering his toast.

"*Why* isn't my breakfast on the table?" he said. "I told you I have an early meeting."

Mom's face turned red. I think he embarrassed her in front of Lee. My sisters' faces often turned red like that when Dad yelled at them.

"Bob," my mother answered in a trembling voice, "you said nothing about an early meeting or breakfast this morning. Am I supposed to read your mind?"

"Why the hell do I have to wait for anything around here? Who do you think supports this family? The least you can do is make breakfast on time."

My mother struggled to find her words, and I knew how that felt. I sometimes couldn't think of what to say when my father raised his voice. Across the room, Lee sat upright in a chair at Mom's desk, her gaze fixed on Dad, and once again I worried that whatever Lee was thinking might make her leave us. I watched Lee's eyes squint and her jaw clench as she watched my mom. Everybody in the kitchen was quiet as Mom placed the eggs in front of Dad. He surveyed the meal, a crease forming in his brow. Then he pushed his chair back from the table, and it made that awful screech again. "Goddammit! These chairs need pads under them!" He snatched up the newspapers and stormed out of the room and out the front door, which he slammed with a boom that echoed through the house like a gunshot. His car tires squealed as he sped away. On the table in front of all of us sat his untouched eggs, toast, and lineup of full juice glasses.

No one said a word.

3

On Lee's first day with us, I taped a blank piece of paper to the lower part of the refrigerator and wrote the number one. Every day that followed, I scrawled the next number in sequence, and when I wrote the number eleven, I knew Lee had been with us for almost two whole weeks. I trailed her day and night, watching her work and asking her questions. That evening, Lee stood at the sink, bent forward scrubbing a dirty pan. I tilted my head, hoping I might be able to catch sight of some special cleaning tricks. "How did you learn how to clean so well?" I asked.

"My older sister, Hazel, taught me. She used to say, 'It doesn't matter what you decide to do, as long as you do it well.'"

"Where is Hazel now?" I asked.

Without turning to face me, she said in a stern voice, "We have a lot to do now. There's no time for questions."

I felt a jolt of fear in my stomach. I'd just asked Lee about her family! What she said next convinced me I'd blown it. I'd ruined everything.

"Tomorrow I'm leaving to spend the weekend in Chicago, where I live."

"Are you coming back?" I asked quietly.

SANDRA SCHNAKENBURG   37

She looked down at me with warm eyes. "I don't know, honey. I haven't made up my mind."

Why hadn't she made up her mind? What had we done wrong? Did Mom give her too much work? Did she not like Dad? Was *I* the problem? Did I ask too many questions?

I slunk into the family room where my parents reclined in armchairs, their feet resting comfortably on the elevated footrests. Between them was a white marble table with a glass of ice water for Mom and a Diet Pepsi for Dad. They didn't seem to notice me as they watched his favorite television show, *Get Smart*. During a commercial, Mom turned to Dad. "Tomorrow Lee's two-week trial is up. I'm afraid she might not want to continue with us."

My father had a quick answer for everything. "Just ask her if she's coming back." My mother didn't reply, so he added, "When you drop her off at the train station tomorrow, just ask her. Doesn't that make sense? Then you won't wonder anymore."

"Good idea."

The next morning, Mom read the train schedule while Lee puttered around the kitchen. With a bright, sunny tone, Mom said, "Lee, there are three express trains on Friday: three fifteen p.m., four thirty, and five thirty. The other options have too many stops. Which one do you prefer?"

"Thank you, ma'am. If it's okay with you, I'd like to catch the three fifteen."

Mom looked up from the schedule, and I knew she was thinking what I was thinking. Lee had chosen the earliest train. Was that bad? Was Lee finished with us?

That afternoon, Robin, Barb, and I climbed into the station wagon. Mom carefully placed Rob in his car seat, and we all sat quietly. The entire inside of the car felt like sadness. As we rode to the train station, I fought to keep tears from falling from my eyes, and when they welled up, I pretended I was scratching an itch. Was this the last time I'd see my new friend who made me feel so smart and helpful? Was the wonderful lady who had made Mom smile again going away forever, and was it because my dad was so mean?

When we reached the train station, we all piled out of the car. Mom pulled Rob from his car seat, and Lee followed her into the ticket office.

Barb shouted, "Let's put a penny on the tracks!" I ran to her and placed my penny next to hers. Then Lee walked out of the ticket office, and I ran back in her direction and wrapped my arms around her legs.

"I'll miss you," I whimpered.

"I'll miss you too, sweetheart."

Mom pulled me off Lee's leg and said, "Let's give Lee some space, dear." Then, bouncing Rob on her hip, she looked at Lee. "Will you let me know if you'll be coming back on Monday?"

Lee looked down and said, "Yes, Mrs. Krilich. I just need some time to think over the weekend."

"I want you to know the children and I truly enjoyed having you stay with us. We'll all miss you very much this weekend, and we hope you'll come back." *Good job, Mom*, I thought.

"Thank you."

The rumble of the incoming train grew louder, its headlight big and bright. Then came a big screeching sound that made me slap my hands over my ears. I looked away from the train and down the tracks to where pretty pink and white flowers bloomed as far as I could see. The wind was warm against my cheeks.

The train finally came to a stop, and people carrying bags and suitcases stepped off and into the sunlight. Smiling people ran down the platform and wrapped disembarking passengers in big hugs. Then a man in a uniform shouted, "All aboard!" and once again I grabbed Lee's leg. She rubbed the top of my head, then climbed up onto the train, and the five of us stood watching as the train started to chug away. From her seat at the window, Lee smiled and waved at us.

"It's okay, honey," Mom said, resting her hand on my shoulder. "Lee probably just needs some rest."

As the train picked up speed, a scurry of wind sent our hair flying around and blew little clouds of dust into the air. Barb and I stepped up to the tracks and rescued our flattened copper pennies. We held them in our hands and walked back to Mom.

I held up my long, flat, smooth piece of copper and said, "Look, Mom, look what the train did to my penny!"

"Make a wish, honey."

I scrunched my eyes closed and wished Lee would come back and stay forever.

For the next two days, Mom spoke very little about Lee. In fact, that weekend she hardly spoke at all. It reminded me of when our dog, Silver, died and everyone was so sad we didn't talk to each other, just moped around.

On Monday morning, all of us except Robin were in the kitchen eating breakfast. The atmosphere was relaxed because

Dad wasn't there, but we were all still pretty quiet. Then the phone rang.

"Hello," said my mother brightly, although I knew that was her fake phone voice. Since Lee had stepped on the train last Friday, Mom hadn't laughed once, and she'd barely smiled.

"I understand. Yes, thank you for the call," she said, and hung up.

Oh wow, this was it. She was about to tell us it was all over, that Lee had rejected us.

Mom pressed the button on the intercom. "Robin, come join us downstairs in the kitchen. Hurry. I have news." Robin came running down the stairs, and I tried to read the expression on Mom's face. Was she disappointed? I couldn't tell.

"Kids, that was the agency that sent Lee to us. They said Lee did a lot of thinking over the weekend—"

"And she's going to live with us!" squealed Barb.

"Let me finish, dear," my mother said. "The agency tells me Lee has agreed to come for two more weeks."

We all sat there, confused. I said, "Didn't she already come for two weeks?"

Mom smiled. "That was a two-week commitment, and now Lee has agreed to another two-week commitment. This is a smart decision on her part. It's wise to make sure you're ready before you decide about important things. It's wise to give a situation thought before you make promises."

I couldn't think of any decisions that could need more than a day to figure out, but so what, Lee was coming back! And that meant that for at least two more weeks, Mom would be happy again.

Two hours later, Mom, Rob, Robin, Barb, and I waited on the train platform. My sisters stayed home in their bedrooms, where they liked to spend a lot of their time. I thought they were crazy to miss this. Mom looked up and down the train track and said it was safe for Barb and me to lay our pennies down to be smashed by the next train. This time I kissed mine first and wished for Lee to move in and stay with our family forever. I hoped Barb wished for the same thing. We needed as much wish power as we could get. Then we scrambled back to Mom and waited.

The train screeched into the station, and as people began to step down onto the platform, I jumped again and again trying to see over all the grown-ups. Every time I saw someone with black hair, my heart leapt, until finally there she was.

"I see her, I see her!" I yelled.

Lee walked toward us, slightly bent forward and still carrying her big Mary Poppins purse. I ran to her and hugged her legs, and she stroked my hair.

"Hello, Sandy," she said, and I could hear she was smiling. Sure enough, when I looked up, I saw her flashing that warm smile with those perfect, straight teeth.

As soon as we arrived back home, Barb and I swarmed her like hungry puppies.

"Okay, children, settle down," Mom said.

Lee hid a prize in each of her hands hidden behind her back. "Close your eyes tightly, no peeking. Now, on the count of three. One, two, three. Open your eyes."

Jumping up and down, we picked a hand and then ripped open the plastic containers that held plastic Cracker Jack prizes inside. Barb got a bracelet, and my surprise was a necklace. We both thanked and hugged her. I loved surprises, and I loved the Cracker Jack prizes because they came from Lee.

The routine of Lee staying for two weeks but not committing continued for months, and each time she came back I believed my penny wishes were working. Summer faded away, and the leaves of the oak and maple trees changed color and fell all over the lawn. Every time Lee came back on a Monday, I asked what she'd done over the weekend, and she always said, "I just rested."

Through big, white snowstorms and then beautiful flowers springing up from the ground, Lee kept leaving and return- ing. And before we knew it, two years had passed. By then, Lee seemed so comfortable with the house and everything in it, she was like one of the family. But Mom said Lee was still committed to only two weeks at a time. Through it all, little Rob went from crawling to walking and running all over the house. Barb turned nine years old and lost interest in collect- ing Cracker Jack toys, but two years after Lee's arrival, Rob and I still couldn't get enough of her. Every day when I left for school, I burned with envy that Rob got to stay home and have Lee all to himself, to hear her kind voice and play games with her.

One day after Dad left on one of his trips, Mom changed some rules. Lee didn't have to wear her white uniform, and she could watch the Cubs on TV whenever they played. Mom also started buying Lee some of her favorite snacks at the grocery store. Her favorites were peanut brittle and caramel popcorn with peanuts.

I was fascinated with just about everything that had to do with Lee, but nothing held my attention more than her smoking habit. At the same time every day, she came up from the basement, started the coffee, settled into a tall chair in the corner of the kitchen, flipped open a crossword puzzle book and a dictionary, and tore the plastic off a box of Pall Mall cigarettes. She reached her fingers into the little red box, slid one long white cigarette out and carefully placed it between her lips, then flicked the lighter, her eyes fixated on the end of the cigarette that glowed hot orange. Then she closed her eyes as she drew a big breath in, waited, and then exhaled, which sent a long gray swirl of smoke reaching up toward the kitchen ceiling. Sometimes she looked away and out beyond the sliding glass doors of the back patio, where she gazed up into the canopy of trees. She was so quiet and focused, it almost felt as if she'd been taken to another world. I tried to catch a glimpse of what she saw in the trees, but all I could see were swaying branches and fluttering leaves.

One morning I sat in the kitchen waiting for Lee to come up from the basement. She was usually upstairs by 7:00 a.m., but on this day at 7:40 a.m. I was still sitting alone at the table. As minutes ticked by, I became more and more nervous that she was sick. No, maybe her alarm had stopped working. No, what if she fell on her way to the bathroom and was hurt? I didn't want to check on her because the basement was her private area, and Mom had made clear it was off-limits.

I watched the clock. When Lee was forty-five minutes late, my heart started thumping. Then I heard the creaking of the basement door, and Lee stepped into the kitchen. Her hair was uncombed and frazzled, her glasses sat crooked on her face, her tired-looking eyes were framed by big circles, and a piece of toilet paper trailed from her left slipper. The most unsettling part was that she looked so strangely dressed. In a mismatched outfit of a blue-and-pink-striped shirt with orange, yellow, green, and white plaid pants, it didn't seem this could be Lee.

"Lee, is everything okay?"

She answered, but it took her what seemed like minutes. "Oh, sweetheart, I just had a bad dream. I'll be okay once I have my coffee."

As Lee started a pot of coffee, I asked, "What was your dream about?"

"It was nothing. I can hardly remember it now."

I was only seven years old, but even I knew that didn't sound right. Something was wrong with Lee, and if she'd had a bad dream, how could she have forgotten it already? The whole scene scared me. What could she have dreamed about so awful it would send her upstairs late and looking a mess?

I knew not to ask her any more questions, so I simply pointed down and said, "There's some toilet paper on your slipper."

Quietly, slowly, she said, "Thank you, honey," and bent over to remove it. That's when I noticed she was shaking, and that scared me. She looked up and must have seen the look in my eyes. She said, "Let's sit down for a minute while the coffee is brewing." Lee walked over to her usual chair in the corner and reached for her box of Pall Malls. She placed a cigarette between her puckered lips and lit it with her Chicago Cubs lighter. She took a long inhale, then paused, and her hands stopped trembling. Then she exhaled a long stream of smoke. I wondered if she dreamed about the car accident that killed her husband and son, but I knew not to ask.

One Saturday not long after Lee's bad dream, I overheard my parents talking in the family room. If I sat on the bar stool next to the wall behind their recliners, I could see and hear them without them knowing I was there. Dad seemed relaxed for a change, as he leaned back in his recliner and sipped a Diet Pepsi after dinner.

Mom said, "Lee has been an enormous help to me, and the kids love her. I wish she didn't have to keep going back and forth to the city. I read about so many muggings—I worry for her safety."

Dad shifted onto his hip to face Mom. "Has she been paying for an apartment all this time?"

Dad talked about money a lot.

"She told me she rents an apartment. But it doesn't make sense for her to waste all that money when she spends so much time here. I'd like her to stay here full-time."

"I agree. Invite her to stay here permanently," Dad said.

This was exciting! Oh, how I hoped Lee would say yes. I wished I could flatten a penny and make a wish.

The next day, I sat at the kitchen table doing homework while Mom worked at her desk. She grabbed a pair of glasses, read something from a piece of paper, and dialed the phone.

My mother said, "Hello, do you rent rooms?" She tilted her head as she listened. Then she said, "Not at this time, thank you," and hung up.

Later, I was clearing the table when I heard Mom and Dad talking in the family room, so I crept to the kitchen door and leaned in to hear.

Mom said, "When I called the number on Lee's application, the lady answered the phone, 'YMCA Homeless Shelter.' I was so surprised I didn't know what to say, so I asked her, 'Do you rent rooms?' She was rather short with me. She said, 'Ma'am, we're a homeless shelter. The people who live here can't afford to rent rooms.' Then she asked if I wanted to stay there or if I wanted to donate. Bob, I think Lee lied to us about living in an apartment."

"So she doesn't have a place to live?"

"It appears not. And I certainly understand why she didn't want us to know the truth. But I don't think she's safe there."

"I agree," my father said. "She should live here. Invite her, but don't let her know you called the shelter."

After dinner the next day, Dad wasn't expected home until late. I sat at the kitchen table with Mom and Lee as they relaxed and engaged in their hobbies. Lee was drinking her favorite drink, an Irish coffee.

Lee worked on a crossword puzzle while Mom cut recipes out of *Good Housekeeping*. The faint sound of the news drifted from the television set above the wall in the kitchen. Mom set the scissors down, then looked up at Lee. "I'd like to talk to you about staying here permanently. Mr. Krilich and I don't think it makes sense for you to keep traveling back and forth to the city or continuing to spend money on an apartment. If that sounds good to you, I'll make sure the kids stay out of your hair on the weekends so you can rest."

Lee blushed and pulled out a Pall Mall. "Thank you for the offer," she said. "It does make sense. Do you mind if I let you know in the morning?"

Lee sure did a lot of thinking about decisions.

The next morning, Lee and Mom sat at the kitchen table sipping their coffee. I was looking in the refrigerator trying to decide what to have for breakfast. Lee cleared her throat and said, "I would like to stay, but I don't want to be a bother, so if you prefer, I can remain in the basement on my days off."

Mother pressed a hand against her chest and shook her head. "Oh, Lee, no. I want you to think of the entire home as yours. It would please me more than anything in the world if you would make this *your* home."

Lee's voice cracked as she replied, "Thank you. I am . . . deeply grateful for you, Mrs. Krilich."

"You're so very welcome, Lee. And the kids are going to be so excited."

I squinched my face and silently screamed—just to myself. My pennies had worked!

$\sim\!\!\sim\!\!\sim$ 4

Appearances were very important to my mother. But even more important to her than having clean kids was making sure her children knew how to clean—her daughters, that is. With Lee staying with us permanently now, Mom felt it was time to teach the kids a thing or two about housekeeping so Lee could have time to rest and not worry about the condition of our house on her days off. Mom had an idea.

One day as Mom unpacked groceries, she asked Lee, "Do you mind giving the children daily chores and teaching them how to thoroughly clean a house? I can offer them a small allowance for their efforts."

"Yes, ma'am," Lee responded. "I'll be happy to teach them, but I prefer to pay them myself since I'm the one they'd be helping."

"Oh no, now you don't worry about paying them. Just be sure they don't operate any dangerous machinery, handle the iron without supervision, or do anything dangerous in terms of heights. I'd love for them to learn as much as possible."

"Yes, ma'am, I'll give them safety tips. We'll always make sure they're safe."

The next day after school, Lee asked Barb and me, "Are you girls ready to learn some household chores?" Barb and I were the only ones available. Roseann and Debbie were high school teenagers with no interest in learning how to clean, and Robin was into boys, music, and art—not much else. In our home, housework was the work of females, so that left Barb and me.

The following day after school, Lee said, "We'll start with your beds. I'm going to show you how to make a bed like a professional, and from now on both of you will make your bed every day. I have some other chores to assign you, and each week after you've finished them, I'll pay you an allowance of a dollar and fifty cents."

I clapped and yelled, "Yay!"

Barb said, "Thank you so much. I sure could use the money."

Lee led Barb and me upstairs to the bedroom my sister and I shared. The pink, purple, and white bedspreads on our queen beds matched the drapes that hung heavily in front of our big, sunny windows. On the wall opposite the beds were four rows of bookshelves stocking volumes of classic fairy tales, Disney stories, books by Robinson Crusoe and Mark Twain, an assortment of Dr. Suess books, and a collection of encyclopedias Mom had bought from a door-to-door salesman. Below the shelves was a full-size television we rarely used, and in the corner under the bookshelves was the laundry chute. One wall was dominated by two mirrored closets separated by an ornate chest of built-in white wooden drawers with gold handles.

On this day our beds had been left untidied. Standing there looking at the blankets and sheets all crumpled and bunched, I thought an unmade bed made the whole bedroom look sloppy, and I wondered if all this time Lee had thought we were lazy.

Lee stood next to my bed first. "Okay, girls, the first thing you do is pull the top sheet and blanket aside, then tighten and tuck the fitted sheet so it's snug over the mattress, like this." She whipped the top layers of bedding over to one side. Then she pulled one corner of the bottom sheet down and tucked it under the mattress. "Then smooth out all wrinkles and creases and make sure the corners are tight and secure under the mattress."

I was dazzled by how quickly she moved and how magically smooth she was able to make the bottom sheet. "Why is it called a fitted sheet?" I asked.

"Sweetheart, because it's made to fit tightly on the mattress. See the elastic corners? But the sheet you pull over your body at night is the flat sheet. Sometimes it's called the top sheet. Here you go, girls. Help me tuck the bottom sheet."

Barb and I got busy pulling and tucking the bottom sheet of my bed.

"Nice work," she said. "Looks good. See how flat and smooth that surface looks? That's what you want. You two are naturals."

Barb and I beamed at each other across the bed.

"Okay, next tuck the bottom edge of the flat sheet tightly under the mattress, then fold the excess fabric at the bottom corner diagonally and tuck it under the mattress. You see? Like this."

Lee yanked my bedspread and arranged it over the top sheet. "To finish, pull the bedspread fully over the flat sheet to the top edge of the bed. Then arrange the pillows upright against the headboard and leave the little pink pillows for last so they can sit out in front."

I'd never imagined there was so much involved in making a bed. What I liked most about working with Lee was she explained everything slowly and never once raised her voice. When we made mistakes, she showed us how to correct them. I was used to trying to learn things from my father, who was usually impatient and made me feel stupid.

Lee stood with her hands on her hips and looked at the bed, then at me. "The stuffed animals can go in front—arrange them however you like."

"I'll do it," I snapped at Barb, and I arranged my panda, giraffe, and zebra animals in a line in front of the pillows.

"And that's that," said Lee.

"Can I go now?" whined Barb.

"We haven't done your bed yet," Lee answered. "A job isn't done until it's done."

Behind Lee's back, Barb rolled her eyes, but she stuck around long enough to help me make her bed.

Lee watched us from start to finish. "This is excellent work, girls," she said. "Now you can both make your own beds each morning before school. Now, who wants to learn how to sweep the kitchen?"

Barb was already on her way out the door when I squealed, "Me!" It was a glorious thing, learning to do grown-up jobs.

Before long, Barb lost interest in learning how to do chores, even if it meant being paid. But I loved learning from Lee, so every day after school, I followed her around the house. I watched how she scrubbed, polished, swept, and ironed, then I tried to copy her movements exactly. She patiently showed me how to transform a rusty faucet into a glimmering fixture by applying steady firm pressure as I scrubbed. She taught me how to vacuum perfect lines on the carpet and to catch every speck of dirt. I learned how to tuck bedsheets so tightly I could make a penny bounce on the mattress. And I learned to polish silver so perfectly I could see my face in the reflection.

Cleaning all the windows in the house took an entire week, so we did it only once a year during the spring. That job turned out to be the hardest of all, but it was the most rewarding because the world outside looked so clear and pretty after we finished.

There were many times while doing chores I made sloppy mistakes, like not being able to reach the top of shelves or get into the corner edges of the outside windows. Other times, I left streaks on the mirrors in the bathrooms or missed some of the chandelier crystals. But even when I messed up, Lee kindly showed me a better way to do the job. She taught with reward, not punishment, and that made me even more motivated to please her. I knew Lee worked for Mom, but I liked the idea that I worked for Lee.

After spending a year and a half shadowing Lee through household chores, there was only one thing I wanted for my birthday. A children's cleaning supply set was constantly being advertised on TV, and I wanted one! It included a broom, dustpan, mop, sponge, bucket, window cleaner, and a feather duster. It even had a kid's "vacuum cleaner" that combed the carpet all in the same direction. And the best part was that the set included a mini-ironing board and plug-in mini-iron.

I'd previously tried using Lee's big iron, but it was too heavy for me, so Lee and I ironed together. She placed her delicate hand over mine and guided the iron smoothly across the wrinkled fabric. Watching the transformation of a wrinkled messy napkin into a flawlessly flattened cloth felt like witnessing magic. Oh, how I wanted that cleaning set.

On the night of my birthday, Mom, Lee, Roseann, Debbie, Robin, Barb, Rob Jr., and I were gathered at the dining table for dinner. The air was warm thanks to the heat from our crackling fireplace, and the irresistible aroma of chocolate cake drifted throughout every room. The house was beautifully decorated for Christmas, and as always, the centerpiece of it all was our gold tree with its bright lights that flashed reds, blues, greens, and yellows.

Earlier that day, I'd gone on a hunt for my birthday present but couldn't find anything in closets, under beds, in the basement. There was no sign of a birthday present anywhere. In past years my birthday gifts had sometimes been placed under the Christmas tree alongside the family's many Christmas gifts, but not this year. Had everyone forgotten about me?

I finished my plate of Mom's homemade spaghetti and sighed. Green and blue balloons hovered behind everyone's chairs, and whenever anyone got up, the balloons seemed to dance and sway. I loved balloons and I loved birthdays, but this year my big day was turning out to be a big dud.

Mom got up to help Lee clear the table, and she returned carrying a big chocolate cake with flickering candles. Lee switched off the lights, and everyone sang "Happy Birthday," just for me. After the singing ended, Lee flipped the lights back on, and Mom handed me the first piece of cake, then served everyone else. Debbie was the first to finish her cake and, somehow, she snuck out of the room without my noticing.

Then she appeared at the far end of the room carrying a huge fluorescent-pink box. It was so big there was no room for it on the table, so Barb hopped up out of her chair.

I looked at Mom. Then at Lee. Then my eyes darted from Mom to Lee. Then I started tearing at the beautiful pink polka-dot paper. When I saw the pictures on the box, I gasped. There it was, my own collection of cleaning supplies!

The next day, Lee and I set up my mini-ironing station next to Lee's big ironing stand. She handed me a wrinkled cloth napkin and watched as I mimicked her ironing techniques. Quickly I became frustrated that I couldn't iron out the wrinkles fast enough, so I tugged Lee's arm. "Why doesn't my iron work like yours?" I grumbled while pressing the iron to my cheek.

Lee snatched the iron out of my hand and snapped, "No! *Never* test an iron on your face! If it were a big-girl iron, you would have just seared your face! Do you want horrifying burn marks on your face?"

My face felt hot, but it wasn't from my toy iron. My iron never heated up as hot as Lee's because it was made for kids, so I didn't understand why she was so upset. Lee had never scolded me before, and my cheeks, ears, and neck burned with shame. Lee's opinion of me mattered more to me than my siblings', my father's, and sometimes even my mother's. That might have been because she paid so much attention to everything I did. Everything I did seemed to matter to her, so I always wanted to get it right. And she was so very kind, always so approving—I just couldn't bear the idea of disappointing her.

A few days later, I hung around the basement as Lee ironed one of my dad's business shirts and listened to a Cubs game on the radio. She was focused and I was bored. I wandered quietly in the direction of the cracked partition that divided the rest of the basement from Lee's bedroom area, the part of the house Mom had always made clear was strictly off-limits. I glanced over my shoulder at Lee, and when I saw her back was facing me, I slipped behind the partition.

In her bedroom, I stared at two little black-and-white photos that sat on her big cream-colored dresser. Standing on my tiptoes, I leaned in to see what I could learn from the faces in the pictures. In one photo was a white man dressed in a military uniform. In the other photo was a young boy with light brown skin and crossed eyes. I guessed he was about two years old. He stood beside a bed, and a crossword book sat on the bedspread. I wondered if this was Lee's husband and son who had been killed.

I leaned in closer on the tips of my toes to get a better look. Then I heard the partition creak open behind me. "What has you so curious, sweetheart?" Lee asked.

A hot jolt shot through my stomach. I knew I wasn't supposed to go in her bedroom, and I knew I wasn't allowed to ask her about the people in the photos. But I'd been caught. So I took a big breath and asked, "Who are these people?" Then I braced myself, half expecting Lee to scold me as my father would have.

She let out a deep sigh, then closed her eyes and tilted her head back. "The man was my husband. He held an important position in the army. And the little boy, his name was Pierre. He was my son."

That's all she said. I was confused because I thought there must be so much more to say, but she stayed quiet. I was also confused because she hadn't scolded me for sneaking into her bedroom. Lee frowned at the photos for a moment and then said, "Come over here, Sandy. Sit with me."

She had a tall bed, much higher than mine, and she lifted me up and placed me next to her on the bed.

"I'm going to tell you what happened to my husband and son, but you need to promise me something first." Her voice seemed to be warning of something dangerous.

"Okay," I answered, turning my head to look at her.

"Promise me you won't ask me about them again."

I really hoped I could keep that promise without blowing it. "I promise."

Lee cleared her throat and held my hand. She crossed one leg over the other and looked down at the floor. Then she spoke in a near whisper. "One day, I was preparing a special dinner for my family. I thought I had green beans at home but realized I didn't. My husband offered to run down to the grocery store. Naturally, my son Pierre wanted to ride with his daddy. On their way home, another car ran a red light. My husband and my boy were killed instantly."

I felt another hot jolt in my stomach. "No!" I cried, and covered my eyes with my hands. When I thought about a little boy being in a car and then pictured that car smashed into by another car—the boy in pain, the boy crying, the boy bleeding—I started crying. But Lee didn't seem upset at all. She sat there and patted my back and after a few minutes quietly said, "It's okay, sweetheart. It's okay to cry. It was a very sad day, but I don't want to talk about it again." Then, just like that, she lifted me off the bed and went back to ironing.

I rushed upstairs and buried my face in my pillow, my tears flowing until I cried myself dry. It must have been a terrifying car accident, and her son and husband must have been in so much pain. I wondered how long ago the accident was, and I didn't understand why she said she never wanted to talk about them again. How could she know that? And wouldn't she want to celebrate their birthdays?

A few hours later, Mom found me crying in my room and said, "Is everything okay? Did you hurt yourself?"

"No, Lee told me about her family's accident. I'm sorry, Mom, but I asked her."

"That's okay, dear. You were curious. But please don't ask her about it anymore, okay? We don't want to upset her."

I sat up sniffling and wiped my eyes. "It's so sad she lost her family."

"Yes, it's very, very sad. But what about this—maybe we can be Lee's new family." Then she kissed me on the head and went back downstairs. Mom never sat around long. There was always something in the house to tend to.

Not long after Lee told me her sad, awful story, I thought of a way to make Lee feel like part of our family. It was the morning of Lee's second Mother's Day with us, and after breakfast I asked Mom, "Is it okay if I make Lee a Mother's Day card?"

"That's a lovely thought," she said. "She's certainly been like a second mother to all of you. I think she'd love that." I looked up and saw my mother's eyes were filled with tears.

In my bedroom, I gathered paper and crayons and drew a picture of our family with Lee right in the middle, all of us stick figures. I colored Lee's hair black and her eyes hazel brown and gave everyone else brown or yellow hair and blue eyes. Then I drew red hearts all around the paper and wrote in a green crayon on top, *We love you, Lee! Happy Mother's Day.*

After Mom opened her Mother's Day cards, I handed Lee the card I'd made. She read it with tears in her eyes. "This is absolutely wonderful, thank you so much."

I hugged her, then hugged my mom.

Whenever Mom and Lee were with me, I knew I was safe. I knew I would be taken care of. But being near my father could mean danger.

~~~~~ **5**

In June 1968, I was six, and very excited about the summer ahead. One Saturday as the sun rose, I could smell the aroma of bacon floating through the house, so I jumped out of bed, brushed my teeth, changed into shorts and a T-shirt, and dashed downstairs. Mom stood in front of the stove wearing a pretty green-and-blue dress that swirled as she moved around the kitchen preparing bacon, eggs, pancakes, and toast. All the kitchen windows were open, and the happy sounds of chirping birds filled the room. Mom's hard work in the garden had made the entire yard—front, back, and sides—look colorful and pretty. Through the kitchen's sliding door, I could see beautiful bunches of yellow daffodils and purple, pink, and white tulips.

I loved days like this. The sky was blue, the sun was out, and I had the whole day ahead of me. I couldn't wait to get outside into the fresh air to find adventure.

After breakfast, Dad, my siblings, and I scattered in different directions while Mom and Lee stayed in the kitchen, fixated on a continuous TV loop of people talking about the shooting of Robert Kennedy. I didn't understand much of what I was hearing, but I knew it was sad, so I just wanted to be outside. I thought I'd look for Dad and watch him work or maybe even help him with whatever he was working on. I walked past the barn toward the garage.

"Dad, are you out here?" I called. There was no answer, but when I entered the garage, there he was, lying on the dusty floor beneath the shade of a tractor next to a bunch of tools. He seemed unaware I was standing there, so I stayed quiet and watched him. He was a smart man who went to work in a suit, but he could also lie on his back on a dirty floor to fix anything. I wondered how he'd learned to do so many things, but I didn't dare ask. I waited and thought, *Soon he'll notice me.*

After a few minutes, he turned his head to one side and looked straight ahead at my white Keds. I took a step back, suddenly afraid he'd yell at me for just hanging around. After a few seconds, he looked up, his eyebrows furrowed. "Is that you, Sandy?"

"Yes," I said softly.

"Can you hand me a wrench?"

Dad wanted me to help him! I glanced over to his huge tool chest, a tall red metal cabinet that looked like a bedroom dresser with a lot of long, skinny drawers. Then I froze. I had no idea what he was asking me for. I turned toward him and said, "What's a wrench?"

Dad dropped his tool on the cement with a clank, pulled himself out from under the tractor's machinery, and rose to his full height. Now he looked like a giant. He smelled dirty. Dust floated from his shirt as he locked his eyes on mine, planting his hands on his hips.

"Are you telling me you're so stupid you don't know what a wrench is?"

I thought I might throw up.

"Goddammit," he barked. "Get out of my way. Go bother someone else."

My heart began to race. A lump formed in my throat, and hot tears ran from my eyes and down my face.

He yelled, "*Go!* You're useless. Get out of here!" and with both hands waved me away, as if he were shooing flies.

I turned and dashed back to the house, wiping my tears as I ran. When I reached the front door, I leaned against it and sobbed. After a few minutes, the door opened, and there stood Lee. She wrapped her arms around me and said, "Sweetheart, are you okay? Are you hurt? What happened?"

Through my gasping sobs, I mumbled, "I'm stupid," and when I heard myself say the words, I cried harder.

With one arm still around me, Lee guided me into the kitchen and reached for a box of tissues on the counter. Then she lifted me onto her lap and rocked me as I cried. Between sobs and hiccups, I tried to share what happened, but it all came out confused and bumbled. Eventually, I blurted out, "I don't know what a wrench is, so Dad says I'm stupid."

Lee gasped. "He said *what*?"

"And he said I'm useless." I looked up and saw an expression on Lee's face I'd never seen before. Her eyes looked like they were full of fire, and her nostrils flared. It was as if she was furious and at the same time trying to beat back the anger to keep from exploding.

She took a deep breath and said, "You can't know something unless you're taught it! He wasn't born knowing what a wrench is! Somebody had to teach it to him. Wait here." Then she gently set me down.

She walked over to the wide drawer in the kitchen where we kept things like scissors and masking tape, grabbed a bunch of tools, and arranged them in a row on the table. She told me the name of each tool, asked me to repeat it, and explained what it was used for.

"This one is a hammer; you use it to bang nails into wood. Maybe you're nailing two pieces of wood together, or maybe you need a nail in the wall so you can hang a picture on it." She went back to the drawer and grabbed some other little metal things, which she laid on the table next to the bigger tools.

"These are nails," she said. "This sharp end goes into the wood, and you can see why, right? It's pointy on this end so it can pierce the wood. And with a hammer, you bang on the flat end."

I nodded, then picked up a tool with a yellow handle. "What's this one?"

"That's a screwdriver. You line it up on the flat end of one of these," she said, holding up a screw. "Then you push and turn. It's another tool that helps you secure something—maybe a piece of wood or metal—to something else."

"I see," I said. And I *was* beginning to see. I liked understanding what these tools were for. After she explained every tool on the table, she mixed them up and asked me what each one was called. Each time she tested me and I got the names and uses right, I felt smarter. I kept glancing at the door, afraid Dad might walk in and see what Lee and I were doing, but he didn't. Now and then I caught Lee glancing coldly out the window in the direction of the garage.

A few months later, I was jumping rope on the edge of our circular driveway. High in the sky, geese were flying in Vs, and

I knew—because Lee had taught me—they were probably soon heading south to avoid a cold winter. The leaves on the trees throughout our yard were just starting to turn yellowish, and under some of them, apples had tumbled to the ground. I happily amused myself with jump rope goals. On that day, I wanted to jump along to the "Mary Mack" rhyme twice all the way through without a miss.

Miss Mary Mack, Mack, Mack
All dressed in black, black, black
With silver buttons, buttons, buttons
All down her back, back, back
She asked her mother, mother, mother
For fifty cents . . .

I was about to finish my second time through when I heard my father's car zipping up the driveway so fast my chest throbbed. When the car was almost at the opening of the carport, it squealed to a stop. I stopped jumping rope and stood frozen as if I'd been caught doing something wrong. Dad got out of the car, slammed the door behind him, and without saying a word grabbed the giant hedge trimmer from the front porch and marched over to where I stood. The closer he got, the bigger the machine's razor-sharp blade teeth looked. He set the monster by my feet and said, "It's about time you stopped wasting your energy on pointless nonsense." He pointed up and down the length of the hedge. "Trim the bushes on both sides of the driveway."

With my legs quivering, I bent down to lift the machine. It was so heavy and bulky, I could barely hold it steady. He showed me how to pull the starter, the vibrations rattling my palms as the chain rotated around and the blades sprang to life. Terrified, I nearly dropped it, but I held on tight because my father's temper scared me more than the angry machine.

He pointed to one end of the bushes. "Start here and work your way to the bottom where the bushes end. After you finish that, move to the other side. Don't come in until you've finished both sides." Then he stormed into the house.

The hedges around our yard were long and extremely overgrown, and I couldn't imagine how I was going to control the heavy machine well enough to do anything but butcher them. I also knew there was a good chance I might cut some of my fingers off.

I gripped the thick handle, then used all my strength to lift the vibrating machine that sent buzzing through my arms and legs and roared in my ears. I took a few big breaths, then started waving the screaming machine across the top of the hedge. Every ten seconds or so, I lowered the trimmer again to catch my breath and summon the power to lift it and wave it a few more times. Now and then, I glanced at the front window and saw Lee watching, a pinched expression on her face. We seemed to silently communicate with each other, *This is not a job for a six-year-old.*

By the time I'd worked my way up and down the length of the bushes, the sun had long set, and mosquitoes were biting every bit of my exposed skin. My arms were almost numb from exhaustion, and my elbows, wrists, shoulders, and neck ached. I snapped the power switch to silence the mechanical monster, walked over to the front patio, and set the machine down. While I'd been working alone in the dark, the rest of the family had eaten dinner without me. But I was excited to show my dad what a great job I'd done. I threw open the front door and found him stretched out in the family room watching television.

"Dad, I finished," I announced.

He got up and walked outside as I scooted to the bathroom off the hallway to wash my filthy face and hands. When I stepped back out into the hall, he was standing there. I was sure he was going to give me a big hug and tell me what a great job I did.

"Sandy, come outside. I want to show you something."

I followed him.

"Look right there." He beamed the flashlight on a section of the hedge. "You missed all those branches." Then he waved the flashlight across another section. "And see all along there? Completely uneven. Looks silly. Fix it tomorrow." Then he went inside.

I was ravenous, but I trudged upstairs without any dinner, ran a bath, and soaked in my tired sadness.

No matter how hard I tried, I couldn't please my father, so after that awful night of straining and struggling and sweating and suffering my way through the awful, unsafe job he'd ordered me to do, I tried to stay far away from him.

But unfortunately for all of us, Dad considered himself in charge. He was the boss, his decisions were final, and if he got himself all riled up about an idea, no matter how unrealistic or reckless, we were all expected to drop what we were doing and get excited about it.

6

In October 1971, Disney World opened its doors. On a Saturday morning five months later, just days before spring break, my father switched on the intercom to make sure his voice blared through the house, "Everybody downstairs. It's time for breakfast!"

What's wrong? I wondered. We all hustled downstairs to the breakfast table, all except Robin, who could probably sleep through a tornado. As Mom hustled around the kitchen serving pancakes, frying bacon, and filling juice glasses, Dad sipped coffee and leaned back in his chair. He glanced over at Rob, now six years old with bright blue eyes and a head full of wavy blond hair. He was a happy kid, and both adults and kids seemed to like him.

"What's new, son?" Dad asked.

"Nothing much," said Rob, shrugging his shoulders. "Except we have next week off!"

"What's that you say?" Dad asked, perking up as if he'd heard some exciting news. "Is it spring break week?"

"Yes, Bob," said my mother while she hustled around the kitchen waiting on everybody. "The kids have next week off. We're talking about a day trip downtown, but mostly the kids just want to stay home."

SANDRA SCHNAKENBURG   67

As we all ate, the room was quiet for a while, but then Dad started shifting around in his chair and scrunching his forehead. I could tell he was thinking up one of his schemes. He finished his meal, slid a cigar between his lips, puckered, and tapped the end of it with a flick of a lighter. As he exhaled, the smoke traveled up in a long ribbon toward the ceiling. Then he reached for the phone and dialed. After several seconds, he said, "Is there availability for eight to Orlando, Florida, today? How many seats are available on that flight? Uh-huh, uh-huh. What about an earlier one?"

I watched my mom's face, her eyebrows twitching and pinching. "Bob, Barb's at a friend's house. They're having a sleepover."

Dad seemed to be pretending my mother wasn't in the room. He said into the phone, "Yes, that will work. Please book eight seats for the noon flight to Orlando." Then he hung up and yelped, "Hurry up, everyone! You have about thirty minutes to pack your suitcases. We're heading to the Magic Kingdom!"

I almost couldn't believe this was happening. Dad got excited about a lot of possible plans, but quite often, nothing came of them. But *this*! We were all scrambling around to pack because we were really going. We were going to Disneyland!

My mother seemed to need to balance herself with a hand on the countertop as she pressed the other hand to her forehead. This was all way too fast. Mom was a careful planner, always organizing hair appointments and outfits weeks in advance, coordinating dresses with shoes, day outfits, and formal attire, down to the smallest accessory. Now, she clutched the sides of her chair and glanced at the clock. Then she jumped out of her chair. "I have to get Barb!" She grabbed her car keys and ran out the door.

Lee got right to work helping us pack. Up and down the halls of the second floor, she called out, "Each of you pick three dressy outfits, shorts, and four tops. Don't forget your swim-suits and toothbrushes." Some of us ran down the basement stairs to look for clean clothes.

Mom arrived home with Barb just as Dad was loading everyone's bags into the back of the wood-paneled station wagon. Lee had already packed a bag for Barb, and I sure hoped it was full of things my sister liked. In the past few years, Barb had started taking her fashion seriously. Mom threw some of her clothes in a suitcase while Dad was honking in the driveway.

As we sped away, Lee stood outside, waving goodbye with a smile. I knew she didn't mind seeing all of us head down the driveway. She always said she loved her time alone.

Dad took the curves on Rainbow Road so fast we were thrown from one side of the car to the other. Driving with Dad always meant somebody ended up gasping or whimpering, and sometimes there was vomiting. My stomach began to gur-gle as the taste of acid crept up my throat.

"Bob, please be careful," my mother said calmly. "We don't want any accidents, do we?" He ignored her and kept swerving.

Barb looked at me. "Sandy, don't throw up!"

Mom looked back at me with sympathy in her eyes. Then she cracked open her window, and a rush of fresh air made me feel better.

When we arrived at O'Hare Airport, we rushed to the Continental Airlines counter where the agent said, "You'll need to step on it if you want to catch your flight," so we all started running. I kept looking over my shoulder, worried Mom wouldn't be able to run fast enough to make it. We were the last to board, and we all flopped into our seats. The plane ride that would mark the start of the vacation hadn't even begun, but we were already worn out.

After we landed in Florida, we headed to baggage claim, then waited and waited for our luggage to roll by. But the belt kept turning, and eventually everyone else from our flight had grabbed their suitcases and left the airport. Dad's plans had been so last-minute, we'd gotten to the airport too late for our bags to be loaded onto the plane.

After renting a car at the Orlando airport, Dad insisted we head straight to Disney World. It was eighty-five degrees and humid, and we were all still dressed in thick sweaters, heavy jackets, and long pants, but when we begged him to let us stop to buy some warm-weather clothes, he said, "Waste of money." So we all trudged through the enormous park dressed for a Chicago blizzard and stood for hours in full sun waiting to board rides.

The hot misery seemed to hit us all at once. "I'm dripping with sweat! Disney World is an oven!" I said.

"Can we *please* buy some shorts or a T-shirt?" Debbie whined.

"Forget it," Dad said. "This place is priced for sucker tourists. Our bags will be delivered soon."

So we all just kept marching from attraction to attraction in our winter clothes, more overheated and miserable by the minute. Mom didn't argue. Her face looked kind of distant and blank.

We eventually made it back to the hotel, and mercifully, so did our clothes. For the rest of the week, Dad ran us all around

Orlando, though my exhausted mother wanted nothing more than to read a good book as she reclined by the pool. By the end of the week, I really missed Lee.

At the end of the trip, we all stood in the hotel's lobby, waiting for a cab. Mom said, "Bob, next time we go on a vacation, I need more notice."

He said, "Okay," but from the grimace on her face, I guessed she didn't think he meant it.

Two months later, Dad and a friend stood behind the bar in our family room clinking crystal glasses and talking about money and travel. I pretended to read on the couch, but I listened. Dad looked sharp in a dark suit, but I thought he seemed like a movie character because of the cigar that dangled from his mouth. Suddenly, he turned toward the kitchen and yelled, "Lillian, what do you think about a quick trip to Puerto Rico?"

Mom scooted in from the kitchen looking like she was on her way to a fancy party, her hair styled so pretty.

"Oh, Bob, I don't know," she said, her hands firmly placed on her hips. "I'd need some time to get ready. When are you thinking of going?"

"Tomorrow!" Dad said as if he'd just announced a great price on a new car. "Just a short trip. Four days to explore the place. I'd also like to ask Mr. and Mrs. White to join us."

Mom looked like she was trying to figure out how to show Dad her anger without looking angry in front of his friend. "*Tomorrow?*"

"That gives you *plenty* of time to pack." He didn't even wait for her to answer. He just reached for the phone and started making reservations. I followed Mom into the kitchen and heard her making rushed phone calls about us kids and our activities. She also tried to fit in a hair appointment, but there were no openings. For someone about to go on a fun vacation in Puerto Rico, she looked frazzled.

Three days after they left, a special delivery box arrived from Puerto Rico. It was all sealed up except for holes on the top and sides. Rob and I couldn't wait to help Lee open the box. What had Mom and Dad sent us from that exotic place?

Lee carefully cut into the tape around the edges, and right away something in the box moved. She jumped back and gasped, "I think there's something alive in here."

That idea thrilled me. "We need to open it and see if it's hungry!" Carefully, I pulled each flap of the wooden box and looked inside. "It's three little crocodiles!" I squealed.

"Wow!" said Rob. "Cool present!"

Lee stepped back from the box. "What in heaven's name are we going to do with crocodiles?"

By now, Robin and Barb had come downstairs to find out what was going on.

"Whoa!" said Barb.

"I hate crocodiles!" said Lee. "I grew up in Louisiana, where they lurk in the marshlands, just waiting to take a bite out of someone."

Robin said, "We have to put them where they won't dry up!" Then she and Barb carried the baby crocodiles to our fishpond just under the stairs to our bedrooms. They were just babies, not much longer than a hot dog bun, so we agreed they should be fine and wouldn't try to go anywhere.

I turned to Lee. "I didn't know you were from Louisiana. Do you still have family there?" I asked.

"No, dear. I have no family left. Now let's stop with the questions." She took the box out to the trash, then went to the patio and lit a cigarette.

Later that evening, the phone rang, and Lee answered it. "Hello, Mrs. Krilich. Yes, the children are fine," said Lee, "but I'm pretty sure your husband is trying to get rid of me!"

From where I sat across the kitchen table, I could hear Mom laughing through the phone, and I inched closer to hear what she was saying. "Oh no, he just wanted to add a touch of the tropics to our fishpond. They're called dwarf caiman crocodiles, and they stay small. They're nothing like big, saltwater crocodiles. People have them as pets here in Puerto Rico. Bob thought it would be a nice addition to our koi pond." Lee's eyes widened as she listened.

Like Rob, I thought the baby crocodiles were cool, and I couldn't wait to tell my friends about them. But Lee never went near the pond.

After a few weeks, the baby crocodiles grew to a foot long and wandered into the part of the pond where the goldfish lived. We didn't pay much attention to the fish or the crocodiles, but once a day, Rob or I sprinkled fish food in their water and watch as they scrambled to eat. After a few more weeks passed, we noticed fewer and fewer goldfish. It upset me that our goldfish were being eaten, but that was only the first of our crocodile problems.

One day Rob said, "Hey! Where are the crocodiles?"

"I don't see them," I said.

"Lee!" Rob shouted. "The crocodiles are gone! All three of them are gone!"

Lee rushed into the foyer clutching a broomstick, the weapon she grabbed whenever she wanted to be prepared to face danger. We looked all around the house, in cupboards, under beds, and in closets, but we couldn't find the crocodiles. For weeks we lived in fear they'd show up at our feet at the breakfast table or come scrambling out from under our beds at night.

In her usual no-nonsense way, Lee said, "Make sure you wear your shoes inside the house at all times."

Having crocodiles, even little ones, inside a family home was a terrible idea, but nobody ever stood up to my dad after he'd announced one of his big ideas. No matter how irresponsible or unsafe or just plain insensitive his big plans were, Mom had modeled "go along with it" behavior we all learned to follow.

Now what were we supposed to do about three crocodiles roaming around inside our house? We didn't really know what to do but try to be careful. Lee never went anywhere without a broom in her hands. The rest of us almost never took our shoes off.

A couple months after the crocodiles went missing, I was reading up in my room, and I heard Lee scream, "Crocodile!"

Barb, Rob, and I rushed to the bar where she held a cocktail glass in one hand and a towel in the other. She stood staring into the cabinet where my parents kept their alcohol and lots of fancy glassware. I tiptoed over to Lee's side and saw two little crocodiles, crunchy and dead, lying belly up, their eyes and mouths wide open.

"They must have dried up searching for water and food," Lee said.

The idea of those poor creatures dying of dehydration made me heartsick. My father was responsible for these deaths!

"They should have just stayed in the pond, dumb reptiles," Rob said.

Lee looked down at him. "They needed food."

"But where's the third one?" I asked.

"It probably died, too, somewhere else in the house," Lee said.

Great. Now we not only were responsible for the deaths of two innocent creatures, a starving one might still be roaming the house. For many months Lee kept a broom close by, and the rest of us continued to walk around the house with our shoes on.

We never found the third crocodile.

A few months after we found the dead crocodiles, everyone but Dad was sitting at the kitchen table for dinner, when suddenly we heard an enormous *bang*!

"What was *that*?" Robin asked.

Lee sprang from her chair and rushed to open the front door. "There's a car fire by the gas pump!" she screamed. "People are on fire, get blankets and water, quick!" She ran toward the flames like a firefighter, and running right toward her was a woman with flames engulfing her back. As they neared the house, I could see it was Mrs. Batista, the lady who lived in the house near the barn on our property. She and her husband took care of our big landscaping projects—like cutting down trees—in exchange for free rent. Her three terrified children trailed behind her, their clothes smoking. It appeared they'd all been inside the car when it exploded.

Lee ripped off Mrs. Batista's sweater and smothered the flames coming from the back of her while the children clung to their mother's legs. They were all strangely quiet. No one was screaming.

Lee took Mrs. Batista's hand and said, "Everything's going to be okay. Come with me." Then she guided her toward the house where Mom was waiting with blankets and water. Mom and Lee laid her down on the blankets in front of the fishpond and poured water over her body as she cried out, "Help me, Jesus!"

The kids lay down on the blanket next to their mother, and I served the three of them water. Barb and I rubbed the kids' backs to help calm them.

Lee ran to the phone and called 911. "Please send an ambulance to Ninety-Two Rainbow Road in Barrington. We have four burn victims here. Car explosion. Please come quickly."

Soon, the sounds of sirens pierced the air. Lee knelt beside Mrs. Batista and kept talking to her. "Help is on the way. You're going to be fine. Just breathe." I watched Lee in awe. How did she know what to do, what to say?

The ambulance raced up the driveway, and two paramedics rushed into the house carrying a stretcher, which they set on the floor before gently lifting the poor lady onto it as she moaned in agony. Then they hustled her out to the ambulance. From the moment the woman came running across our yard until the ambulance disappeared down the driveway, my heart didn't stop thundering. I'd never seen something so frightening in real life.

With tears in my eyes, I turned to my mother. "What happened? Why did that car catch fire?"

"I don't know, honey. We'll wait until your father gets home to investigate."

How was Dad going to know? I wondered. He wasn't home when it happened. Once the ambulance left, we all stood bewildered. Had the car's gas tank malfunctioned? Had someone thrown a lit cigarette near the pump?

Time passed, and we all stopped talking about the car explosion, but I never stopped wondering what really happened that day.

Nearly four months after the explosion, Mom gathered all of us in the family room for a talk. She remained standing while we all sat around her on couches and chairs. "Kids, your father will be going away for a while, but we'll all manage fine without him."

"Going away where?" I asked.

"Your dad is going to prison." She didn't give us time for the information to sink in before she continued. "He wasn't paying the correct amount of taxes to the government, so they gave him a year sentence. I don't think you should tell any of your friends about this."

"Do we get to visit him?" Barb asked.

"Yes, we'll visit him often. But it means you'll see less of your friends during the coming year. We'll be visiting him most weekends."

I was nine years old. My father was going to prison. I had absolutely no idea why my father was going to prison. But once again, we were all bending ourselves around him.

SANDRA SCHNAKENBURG   77

Almost every Friday for the next year, our family packed up the car and drove four hours to a federal prison in Marion, Indiana. Then we spent eight hours every Saturday and six hours every Sunday in a prison visiting room with almost nothing in it but vending machines. On the night in between, we crammed ourselves into one hotel room, all seven of us. Barb, Rob, and I slept on the floor in sleeping bags while Mom and my older siblings shared the two beds. After Sunday's visit, we left directly from the prison and drove four hours to get home, stopping only briefly for fast food. During the ride we all elbowed each other for space as we struggled to do our homework, often ending up nauseated from motion sickness. We usually arrived home around 8:00 p.m., which left enough time for a bath before going to bed. Five days later, we started the entire miserable cycle again.

It was a dreadful year. There were no after-school sports, no sleepovers, no birthday parties, no vacations, just trips to prison to spend time with the father we'd spent almost no time with all the years prior. I don't know what his life was like in between our visits, but every time we saw him, he said he was going to take all of us on a safari in Africa. "Just as soon as I get out," he said. It seemed not even prison life could stop my dad's big ideas.

Finally, the year passed, and Dad had served his sentence. For the first few weeks after his release, he came home after work and ate dinner with us, but then he started staying out late and coming home drunk. He never spoke of Africa again.

With Dad home again, mornings were no longer peaceful. We all had to listen to his complaining—his coffee was too hot or too cold, seven juices weren't enough, and his eggs were overdone. One morning before Dad came downstairs, Mom sat at the kitchen table quietly sipping her coffee and easing into the day. Then my father walked into the room.

"Where's my breakfast? Can't you do anything right?"

Mom's shoulders tensed, then she jumped out of the chair as if startled by an intruder and hurried from the table to the stove. Her voice trembled. "If you give me a few minutes, I'll whip up some eggs and bacon."

"The hell if I'm going to wait! What are you good for anyway?"

My mother placed warm eggs on a plate and set them down in front of him. Lee stood up and said, "Mr. Krilich, it's my fault breakfast wasn't ready. Lillian and I were discussing the schedule today, and I distracted her from preparing your breakfast."

"Then you're both worthless. And Lee, you're fired! We don't need people around here who don't do their job."

Lee just walked away as if she hadn't heard him. By now, her being fired at breakfast and rehired by lunch had become a comical routine.

My father snapped, "Goddammit, why is my coffee not hot?"

Lee said, "Mr. Krilich, the coffee was just made. The temperature should be just right. If it's not, I can remake it for you."

Dad's eyes were full of fire, but he backed off. I think Lee's presence infuriated him because it meant he was no longer free to use my mother as a punching bag. After Dad stormed out of the kitchen and we heard the front door slamming and his car speeding away, Mom and Lee sat and took long, deep breaths. Then Lee said, "Try not to let it get to you. Don't take his criticisms to heart. He's the one with problems, not you."

"Thank you," Mom whispered.

Even as a child, I knew there was nothing wrong with my mother but everything wrong with the way my father treated her and our family. After he got out of prison, I thought he might start acting calmer and nicer. I thought he might have developed a sense of gratitude, maybe come home a changed man. But no. After that year, he became even moodier. He yelled at Mom more, criticized all of us more. I could see it all wearing on our mother. She started looking so very tired. It didn't help that even our sleep schedules could be affected by Dad's lifestyle.

One night, soon after Dad's "you're both worthless" rant, he came home late, long after we'd all gone to sleep. We were all jolted awake by Mom's voice blaring over the intercom.

"Wake up! Your father is home and wants you downstairs. Now."

All six kids stumbled out of bed, bleary-eyed, and shuffled downstairs in our robes and slippers. Mom told us to sit around the table so Dad wouldn't have to eat his dinner alone. It was 10:15. We slumped into our seats and tried to keep our eyes open as our father settled himself in front of a plate of steak, potatoes, and green beans, dropped a napkin on his lap, and began to eat in silence.

Every few minutes I glanced up at the clock on the wall behind where Dad sat. This felt like the longest night of my life. I was exhausted and hazy headed and trying desperately to stay awake to avoid my father's anger, terrified of what might happen to me if I had the nerve to fall asleep as he ate. He kept us all at the table until 11:10 p.m.

The following day, someone from the school called my mother to ask if I was getting enough rest because I'd fallen asleep during reading class. Mom told them she'd make sure I started going to bed earlier, but that was an unnecessary promise. I already had a perfectly reasonable bedtime; the problem was Dad. If he barged into the house late and wanted attention, he was going to get it, and Mom seemed powerless to do anything about it.

That afternoon, I heard Mom telling Lee how embarrassed she was about how rudely my father often talked to both of them. "It's so disrespectful, but I don't know what I can do about it."

Lee said, "Mrs. Krilich, you need to stop reacting to him. If you don't respond, eventually he'll stop."

"I don't understand. You think I should just say nothing?"

"That's right. If a man disrespects you, you don't give him the satisfaction of a response. Do the opposite—stand tall and confident and don't say a word."

"I don't know if I can do that."

"Then walk out of the room. Don't let him see he upset you."

Mom looked up at Lee and tipped her head to the side. "May I ask how you know so much about how to manage a tyrant?"

"I read a lot."

Lee sure did read a lot, but I never saw her do any writing. Still, she claimed to want to write a book. One evening as Mom, Lee, and we six kids sat around the table having dessert, Lee mentioned she had a book idea. She sat at the head of the table in my father's chair and blurted out, "Someday, I'm going to write a book about my life, and no one will believe it!"

We all laughed, and her big statement got lost in the laughter and chatter that usually filled the room when my father wasn't around. None of us asked what her book was going to be about. I think we were all stuck somewhere among curiosity about her past, sadness for her losses, and fear of violating Mom's rule that nobody was allowed to ask Lee about her life. It was a strange position to be in because I really did want to know all about Lee. After she mentioned the book, I leaned in, hoping she'd elaborate, but she didn't. She just grinned and sipped her Irish coffee.

In the years that followed, Lee brought up this "unbelievable" book idea many times, but nobody ever asked her about the specifics. The longer she went without saying a word about her past, the more I grew to suspect there must be something mighty colorful back there to hide. Why else would she keep such a tight lid on it?

7

One of Lee's biggest contributions to our family culture was her passion for baseball. She was one of the Chicago Cubs' biggest fans, and the rest of us lined up with her.

When the Chicago Cubs were playing, we were freed from chores. All household work halted whenever Lee gathered her scorebook, patent leather radio, ashtray, pack of Pall Malls, and Cubs pencil and sat in the corner chair in the kitchen, where she spread everything out on the table in front of her. The television blared the starting lineup, and Lee jotted the name and position of each player and his batting order. Right after the national anthem, she'd explain the intricacies of the game to whichever of us was nearby. From the politics on the field to the subtle messages conveyed by a pitcher's movements, she knew all about it.

One afternoon, I sat next to Lee in front of the television, eager to learn as I watched the game. The pitcher wound up to throw a pitch but then turned and threw the ball to the first baseman. "Why did the pitcher fake out the batter?" I asked.

"Sweetheart, he's not really faking out the batter but trying to prevent a steal. The runner on first is trying to steal second base."

"What are the pitcher's and catcher's hand signals for?"

"It's their secret language. Isn't it exciting to watch? You never know what those two are cooking up."

"Why is there a guy standing between second and third base, but there isn't one between first and second?"

"That guy is the shortstop, and his position is very important. A lot of players bat righty, so they're more likely to hit the ball to the left."

I often didn't understand Lee's explanations, but I loved listening to her. I wondered if I'd ever be as excited about anything as Lee was about baseball.

Lee occasionally asked my mother's permission for Barb, Rob, and me to play hooky from school so she could take us to a game at Wrigley Field. Mom always agreed, and I think it was her way of trying to sweeten our lives after we'd become the children of a convict.

My brother and sister and I had to restrain our giggles the first time Mom called the schools explaining her children had come down with a fever. Then she dropped the four of us at the train station where we caught a ride to Wrigley Field. We were armed with bedsheets we'd spray-painted with bold blue and red letters: Go Cubs, Go, a message meant to catch Mom's eye as she watched the game on television. Lee dressed for games in full red, white, and blue "Spirit of the Cubs" attire that included a Cubs hat and a Cubs pin fastened to her collar. She carried a scorecard, her brown radio, and a Cubs pencil.

As we roamed Wrigley Field, Lee showered Barb, Rob, and me with endless generosity, paying for the game tickets, scoreboards, Cubs pencils, popcorn, peanuts, and hot dogs. She'd also paid for our train tickets to get there. We all understood what a big deal a day at Wrigley Field was to her, so we were on extra good behavior. Inside the park, Lee trudged along with that clunky gait of hers, and we trailed behind her like little chicks until we finally settled into the first row near first base. In front of her on the cement wall she arranged her caramel popcorn, peanut brittle, and radio.

After the national anthem, Jack Brickhouse, the renowned Cubs announcer, introduced the batting order, then the game began. As Jack's voice boomed across the stadium describing the play-by-play, Lee kept her radio tight against her ear so she wouldn't miss a word or call. Before long, Ernie Banks was on deck warming up, at which point Lee sat up straight and kept her eyes fixed on the player she considered the greatest in baseball history. He stepped up to the plate, and it was strike one, strike two, and then announcer Jack Brickhouse's voice boomed over the intercom, "That's a hit . . . back . . . back . . . Hey hey, and it's a home run!" The fans roared. We all jumped out of our seats and sang the words Lee had taught us, "*Go Cubs, Go! Hey, Chicago, what do you say? Cubs are gonna win today!*"

During the seventh inning stretch we all sang, "Take Me Out to the Ball Game," and Lee shouted, "Louder! The players need to hear you sing!" I don't even remember if the Cubs won or lost that day. The thrill was being in Wrigley Field with the most passionate fan of the Chicago Cubs.

Back when Dad was in prison, Mom's sister Diane came to live with us and sparked the household with a new kind of dynamic energy. We played a lot of games, told jokes, laughed, and ate pizza, hamburgers, and hot dogs. Sometimes we even piled into the station wagon and went to the glorious place called Burger King. I think it was clear to all of us that our home without Dad in it was a lighter place.

Auntie Di was kind of kooky, and having her around was sometimes like living with a whacky movie character. She often said she was very spiritual and could "feel things" and even referred to herself as a psychic. Sometimes when one of my girlfriends stopped over, she'd bend her index finger toward her and say in a creepy, deep voice, "Come over here, little girl, and I'll tell your fortune." Aunt Di's ratted flaming red hair gave her a weird, exotic look, and my friends were easily lured. She'd open the girl's hand and swirl her first two fingers around the perimeter of her palm, identifying her life line and marriage lines, then declaring how many children she would have. She'd make predictions like, "You're going to have a long life and marry an extremely handsome man. You will have four children, and one of them will have special gifts."

Whenever Lee was around for one of these fortune-telling sessions, she rolled her eyes, but she got really fired up whenever the Cubs lost by a narrow margin and Auntie Di said it was because the team was cursed.

"I don't believe in curses," Lee always said, even though the day after a Cubs win, she wore the same socks she'd worn the day of the game. When we teased her about being superstitious, she said, "I don't believe in that silly stuff, but I can't take any chances."

I couldn't tell if Lee liked Aunt Di or not. They seemed to get along pretty well over long games of Scrabble as they chain-smoked as if they were hours away from their executions. But whenever Aunt Di went off on some of her woo-woo stuff, Lee seemed to find her silly or irritating, like that year on Lee's birthday when Aunt Di insisted on reading Lee's horoscope. It described her as impulsive, stubborn, and unpredictable, which made no sense because Lee was none of those things. This confused me because Aunt Di's horoscope readings seemed to describe all of us accurately.

"That stuff is utter nonsense," Lee snapped.

"You're neither a Capricorn nor an Aquarius! I'm certain of that," said Aunt Di.

Lee stood up and shook her head. "I've had enough of this." Then she marched to the other side of the kitchen and lit a cigarette.

How strange, I thought. Lee really seemed angry.

As the seasons passed, so did the Cubs losses, each one more absurd and extraordinary than the last, further fueling the mystical narrative of the fairy tale of *the curse*. There are several variations of the legend of Billy Goat Tavern owner William "Billy Goat" Sianis and the curse he supposedly cast upon the Chicago Cubs during the 1945 World Series, but the heart of the story is Sianis tried to bring his goat into the ballpark and was turned away. He appealed to Cubs owner P. K. Wrigley himself, but Wrigley said the goat wasn't allowed in because "the goat stinks." At that, Sianis declared the Cubs wouldn't win another World Series as long as his goat wasn't allowed inside the park. The Cubs went on to lose that World Series to the Detroit Tigers, and many believed it was because the curse had taken hold. After that, the curse appeared to vex the team for decades. During several important games, weird events happened, like the time a black cat walked on the field or the day bolts of lightning shot from a blue sky. For countless fans, the curse was always to blame.

Lee swore, "Curses are ridiculous fictions preying upon gullible fools and the feebleminded." Still, the day after a win, Lee always wore those "game-winning socks."

After every season, Lee added another Rawlings Simplex scorebook to the pile of her baseball record keepers that dated back to 1965. Each book documented the player lineup and every play of the game, including every statistic. Lee was tireless when it came to documenting every hit, out, RBI, and home run of her beloved players, and every year she added game pins and buttons and other collectibles to her shrine of Chicago Cubs memorabilia. Her bookshelf was lined with books about Cubs players, and her collection included *Ernie Banks: Mr. Cub and the Summer of '69*, by Phil Rogers; *Billy Williams: My Sweet-Swinging Lifetime with the Cubs*, by Billy Williams; and *Ron Santo: A Perfect 10*, by Pat Hughes and Rich Wolfe. Above Lee's bed hung her most treasured piece of memorabilia, a signed picture of Ernie Banks.

In the off-season, Lee tolerated the lack of baseball by reading romance novels and watching movies and TV shows, eagerly marking her schedule for the week in the *TV Guide*. She kept her mind engaged with crossword puzzles and Scrabble games.

One day after school, I found Lee in the kitchen, engrossed in filling out a form.

"What are you doing?" I asked.

"I am about to become a *lifetime member* of the Chicago Cubs Die-Hard Fan Club," she said.

This sounded like a very exciting group. "Can I be a member?" I asked.

"Oh, sweetheart, I was hoping you'd ask. I happen to have an extra application right here." She slid the paper across the table with a warm smile.

I hopped into a chair and started writing.

Part Two

Fall

"Autumn is the hardest season.
The leaves are falling, and they're falling like
they're falling in love with the ground."

ANDREA GIBSON

$\sim\!\!\sim\!\!\sim$ 8

After my father failed to charm the family at Disney World, he took an entirely different approach to our family vacations. He decided we needed a yacht.

It was the spring of 1972 when the family learned we'd be spending the upcoming summer sailing on the *Robert R*, a vessel my father named after himself. One night at dinner, he asked my mother, "When do the kids get out of school for the summer?"

"Their last day is the Friday after Memorial Day weekend."

Lee looked past my father and said to my mother, "I've already bought eight Cubs tickets for the Tuesday after school is out, and I'm planning to take Barb, Sandy, and Rob, plus their cousins. Whatever you're planning, please make it after this day. The Cubs are playing the Braves, and it's Ron Santo Day. We can't miss this game!"

"We won't interfere with your plans," Mom said.

"Well, I asked you months ago and the children are looking forward to it, as am I," Lee explained with sweat bubbling up on her forehead.

"I can't wait to go to the Cubs game!" I said.

"We're going to sail the Great Lakes on the *Robert R*," Dad said, ignoring Mom, Lee, and me. "It will take two months. I'm arranging for the captain to bring the boat up the Atlantic coast from Florida through the Saint Lawrence River. We'll board in New York City and head up the Hudson River and Erie Canal, through Lake Ontario, stop at Niagara Falls, then continue through Lake Erie, Lake Huron, and Lake Michigan."

This was my father's dream trip, a grand adventure that would span two whole months and during which we'd all celebrate my parents' twenty years of marriage. As he announced his big plans, my mother kept her head down and fidgeted with her knife and fork. Then she looked at him with wide eyes. "Bob, I don't know how to swim."

"It's a Christianson Yacht, one of the best made, and there will be enough life preservers for everyone on board. You'll be fine."

I worried about Mom. By this point, we were all strong swimmers except for her. I couldn't imagine how scary it would be out on a big body of water without knowing how to keep myself afloat. It was another example of Dad's dismissiveness. He had a big idea, and nobody's objections were going to get in the way; not even his own wife's very valid fears made him stop to think.

Mom wasn't giving up. "But that's a long time away, and I'm not sure we should leave Lee home alone that long."

"Lee has been with us for seven years. She can handle the house."

Ever since hearing my father's plans, which we all knew were about to crash headfirst into her plans for a day at Wrigley Field, Lee had been standing at the far end of the kitchen, frowning.

"When are you planning on leaving for this two-month voyage, Mr. Krilich?" Lee asked.

"Can Lee come?" I interrupted.

Her eyes flew open wide. "Oh no, I'd rather stay here and watch over things."

"Oh, please, Lee. It'll be fun!" I begged.

"I'll be very happy to have the house all to myself. And someone needs to take care of the dogs. Plus, I don't particularly enjoy boats, planes, or cars. I'll miss all of you," she said. "Send me lots of postcards."

My poor, weary mother tried to sound positive. "Of course, yes. We'll all send postcards, right, kids?"

"Yes! We'll send a postcard from every place we visit, especially Niagara Falls," I said.

Then in a surprising moment of cooperation, Dad said, "We'll leave mid-June, a week after the baseball game. How's that sound?"

"That works for me," Lee sighed with relief.

We weren't leaving for another two weeks, but I already felt the heaviness of going away for so long without Lee. I got up and hugged her, and she whispered, "I'm trusting you to make sure nobody sends me any live animals."

On a hot afternoon in mid-June 1972, we arrived by plane in New York City and took a taxi to the dock. The first thing I noticed after stepping onto the deck of my father's sixty-three-foot yacht was a plaque of the Krilich coat of arms mounted on the starboard side entrance. We couldn't miss it. It was gold, blue, and red, and at the bottom of the plaque were the words *generosity, truth,* and *loyalty.* In the middle of the emblem were three separate arms holding swords, signifying a family of warriors. Warriors, I thought. Definitely some truth in that.

"All aboard!" Dad yelled before pulling away from the dock.

The sun sparkled on the water, and after watching for a few minutes as the wake ruffled behind us, I went up to the helm where my father was studying several maps. "Dad, can I see the map of where we're going?"

He pointed to New York City. "Here's the starting place. The other colors signify places we'll dock to fuel up, have dinner, and sleep. Everything is planned out." He smiled and puffed his cigar. "You'll see some wonderful places this summer," he said, studying the itinerary. Dad loved adventures, and I knew he wanted this trip to go smoothly. I loved seeing him get all fired up about excursions like this. Dad was always pleasant and chatty when he was at the start of something adventurous and risky, and he loved the energy of having people around, especially when he was the one who had made the event happen. I was just happy to see my father happy.

With a finger, I traced the red line on the map from New York to Lake Ontario and westward through Lake Erie, Lake Huron, and Lake Michigan and finally to our destination, the Chicago Yacht Club. It looked like a crazy long cruise, and I didn't like the idea of going so far and being away from home for so long. I already missed Lee. But I also liked trying new things and seeing new places, so I decided to give into the unknown and enjoy the adventure.

The first week and a half was peaceful. We sailed up the Hudson River and through the Erie and Oswego Canals, then cruised across Lake Ontario toward Lake Erie. Dad had explained that Niagara Falls was formed by the Niagara River, where Lake Erie drains into Lake Ontario and creates the highest flow rate of any waterfall in North America. It sounded thrilling, and I couldn't wait to see this mighty wall of falling water.

By the time we approached our dock a few miles from Niagara Falls, we were all exhausted from the long day on the water, and the long process of docking the yacht only added to our impatience and grumpiness. All six kids acted as crew, following Dad's commands to "Let the buoys out!" "Throw the rope!" "Pull the boat closer!" It was 10:00 p.m. by the time we sat in a restaurant and ordered dinner, and we were all practically falling asleep at the table, but I could tell Mom felt better than she had all day. Her fear of drowning must have made our boat trips excruciating, but she always went along like a good sport.

Early the next morning, we caught a taxi to see the falls up close. There it was, the most extraordinary thing I'd ever seen. I stood in silent awe as I watched the massive wall of water flow gracefully downward, then hit the base of the Niagara River with force so booming I could feel it in my chest. I was fascinated by the power of the water, and I loved hearing Dad explain the facts about this wonder of the world. He said the falls dropped more than 160 feet before hitting the water below. I knew I couldn't fully understand the power of it, but I thought it was really cool that Niagara Falls produced over four million kilowatts of electricity that was used by both the United States and Canada.

I wanted to linger there for hours and daydream about the astonishing natural spectacle, but Dad hustled us away. He was on a schedule, so after watching the falls for only twenty minutes, we went back to the boat, where we untied the ropes and pulled away from the dock, leaving a trail of diesel fuel behind us.

We sailed through the Soo Locks, which Dad said had been created in the mid-to-late 1800s to allow shipping vessels to pass through the Great Lakes. I stood near him up on the bridge and listened to him talk about how the locks worked. "They bring boats up to a new elevation by using gravity in a locked chamber area," he said, his eyes sparkling. I wasn't interested in the subject, but there were so few circumstances during which my father was patient with me, I stayed and asked questions. But as usual, it wasn't long before he became irritated and started giving me sharp one- and two-word answers, so I went down to the galley.

Shortly after lunch, Dad piloted the boat into the first Soo Lock, which landed us in an enclosed chamber surrounded by four slimy brick walls. A deep rumbling followed by a loud beeping signaled a gate had locked behind us.

Dad ordered, "Barb! Sandy! Go to the starboard side and push the boat away from the wall. Robin! Rob! Go to the stern and push the boat away, now!"

We pressed our hands against the slimy green fungus, pushing and pushing until our hands and arms were numb. After about thirty minutes, Barb and I were exhausted, but we had to keep pushing because whenever we stopped, the boat drifted back toward the wall, and neither of us wanted to know what Dad would do if we let his precious vessel hit the sides and get scratched or dented. Slowly the lock filled with water and started to raise the boat.

We pushed the boat from the wall for almost two and a half hours in oppressive heat and thick humidity, and Dad never stopped yelling, "Push it away, harder, push harder!" And finally the lock was filled with water, and our boat had risen three hundred feet.

We kids dreaded every lock after that experience, even though none of them were as slimy as the first one. Every time we entered another lock, Dad was always frazzled and screaming until we'd risen and made our way out. It made me wonder what it was about this kind of journey he found so enjoyable.

During the next two weeks, Dad seemed relaxed. He seemed more confident at the helm, and he'd stopped barking orders. The rest of us settled into our new lifestyle that was dominated by helping Mom prepare breakfasts and lunches, reading, and playing games.

There were long periods of smooth sailing, when Dad could sit back and let the boat just cruise along. One morning he put the yacht on autopilot and headed down to the galley. Barb and I were just finishing breakfast, but we stuck around and made small talk with Dad. He started telling us about the hundreds of waterfalls he'd read about in and around the Great Lakes when, in mid-sentence, he glanced out the window and his eyes popped open wide. Barb and I whipped our heads around to see what had shaken him, and we gasped. A massive oil barge was coming straight for us.

"Goddammit!" Dad shouted. He slammed his cup on the table, which sent hot coffee flying all over the little kitchen.

Then, with Barb and me right behind him, he sprinted up to the helm, where he grabbed the boat's steering wheel and spun it sharply in the opposite direction of the barge.

"Harder, Dad, turn it harder!" Barb yelled.

Dad shouted, "It's going to hit us. Hang on tight, everybody!"

But it was too late. There was a long, intense screeching sound, followed by an enormous *thump,* and then the boat started to tip to the left. And it kept tipping and tipping. The barge had smashed into the port side of our boat and ripped a gaping hole in the bow. Our boat was sinking.

Robin and Rob ran up to the helm and gripped the railings to keep from being thrown into the water. Roseann and Debbie were in the saloon in the rear of the boat hanging on to a railing. By now the boat was nearly on its side.

"Where's Mom?" Rob yelled.

I hurried downstairs and gasped at the sight of water gushing from the master stateroom. Mom was inside and she didn't know how to swim! I rushed to where she stood frozen with her eyes wide open. She was dressed only in her underwear and seemed to be gasping for air out of pure panic.

I called out to my siblings, "Hurry! Come help Mom!" My mother seemed frozen, her mind unable to communicate with her body that she needed to move it.

Roseann and Debbie ran downstairs. The boat was now swaying back and forth, and Mom was thrown against a wall. Something sharp had gashed her knee badly, and blood was running down her leg.

I grabbed her robe and a towel, and shouted, "Mom! Fast! We have to get out of here!"

The water rose fast, gushing through a gaping hole under the stateroom window, and before long it had risen higher than our ankles. Mom was trying to wriggle into a cotton dress she'd pulled over her head, and I yanked it down for her, then grabbed her arm and pulled her into the hallway and up the stairs.

We made it to the top where Dad was radioing for help. "We have an emergency! Our boat has been hit by an oil barge, leaving a gaping hole in the port side. Water has flooded the lower levels. We need immediate assistance." He listened for several seconds, then he turned to us. "The Coast Guard is on their way to pick us all up and get us to dry land. They're going to tow our boat to the closest shipyard, which is in Newark. We'll take our things off the boat and check into a Newark hotel and stay there until the boat is fixed."

Mom shook terribly for what felt like an hour, and her wide-open eyes made her look a little crazy. When members of the Coast Guard arrived, one of them wrapped a blanket around her until she calmed down enough to be transferred into the Coast Guard's boat. Eventually, three Coast Guardsmen guided her off the boat, two of them holding her hands and one pressing a hand to her back as she shuffled down the plank and then stepped onto the safety boat.

Dad leapt right into business mode, calling boat repair places and hotels. He found us a place to stay near the shipyard. By the time we arrived at the hotel, the Coast Guard had already investigated the accident and confirmed it hadn't been Dad's fault. We'd been hit because the barge's lookout man hadn't been at his assigned post. My father was relieved he wasn't financially responsible for the repairs but complained and complained about the inconvenience of it all. Surrounded by six rattled kids and a wife who was still shaking because she thought she'd just escaped a near drowning, he could only say, "Goddammit, thanks to someone else's stupidity, we're completely off schedule."

I looked at my mother with pity. She looked so lost.

The night of the accident, Dad said he had business to take care of in Chicago, so he left us all in New Jersey. Mom desperately wanted to go home, but Dad insisted we all stay and wait for the repairs to be done. It took over a week to fix the massive hole on the side of the yacht and the water damage to the boat's interior, and while we waited, we were landlocked in Newark, surrounded by pollution-spewing smokestacks. The hotel's concierge warned us not to wander around the area because it was riddled with crime, so Mom and the six of us kids stayed in the hotel room, playing games and working on puzzles.

I was still excited about visiting new places along the journey to Chicago, but I knew Mom was dreading the rest of the trip. We still had six weeks ahead of us.

Right after the accident, Mom called Lee and told her all about it. Then she called us kids to the phone so we could say hello to Lee. We all shouted, "We all miss you, Lee! We wish you were here!"

She said, "I miss you too!" but I had a strong feeling she was glad she hadn't come with us.

A few days later, Mom called Lee again, and I hovered near the phone so I could hear Lee's voice. Mom said, "As I'm sure you know by now, Bob went back to Chicago to do business right after the crash. I hope you weren't shocked when he showed up at the house."

Lee was silent for a few seconds, then she said, "Mrs. Krilich, I haven't seen your husband since you all left for the cruise."

Mom's face went white. Then she said, "Oh, he's probably staying in the city at one of the townhouses he built near the office."

Lee didn't reply, and the silence between them seemed to contain an entire conversation.

After a week, the boat was fully repaired, and Dad flew back East to captain the rest of the journey. The days of sailing were long, and we had beautiful, clear weather in which to explore new cities, where we wandered and shopped and ate in exotic restaurants. Barb and I became confident navigating the rest of the Soo Locks as we traveled through Lake Erie and past Detroit into Lake Huron, then through Lake Michigan and past Milwaukee, until finally we pulled into the marina of the Chicago Yacht Club. The sight of the majestic skyscrapers and lakefront beach sent a joyful rush through my body. We hauled our suitcases and all the food off the boat, helped Dad wash down the exterior, then stripped the beds and threw the dirty sheets in the car. After we finished our boat chores, we went out for Chicago-style, deep-dish pizza. It felt great to be back in our home city!

After a one-hour drive to Barrington, we pulled into our driveway, and when the car stopped, I jumped out, ran into the house, and wrapped my arms around Lee. Within seconds, the rest of my siblings ran in and threw their arms around her too. We'd all been aching to be home, and knowing Lee was waiting there to greet us made the homecoming warm and joyful. Most of my siblings ran upstairs to unpack, but Barb and I drifted into the kitchen with Lee, where we sat at the kitchen table telling her all about the trip.

Later as I unpacked in my bedroom, I thought about the two months my family had just spent together. During the second segment of the journey, Dad had seemed more attentive to my mother. Now and then he surprised her with a drink or by asking her what kind of restaurant she preferred for dinner. It was as if after the accident, he'd remembered his wife was along for the trip. I thought about how many different dads I seemed to have, so many different personalities within one person, and I realized the trip had been a good example of who he was in all our lives. He'd whisk us away from the isolation of our life in the suburbs and fill the air with excitement, adventure, and the signature charm he turned on so quickly when he wanted to. But when things didn't go his way, he withdrew from us and stayed silent and focused until he solved the problem.

I never heard Mom ask Dad where he'd been all week after the accident, but where *had* he been? If he hadn't slept at home in Barrington, where had he stayed? Were those townhouses near his office even furnished?

After our Great Lakes adventure, my dad decided to dock the *Robert R* at the Key Largo Ocean Reef Club in Florida. Most of our family time was spent on land now, except for a once-a-year excursion to the Bahamas on the *Robert R* for a week of beach time and fine dining for all of us and gambling for Dad. Many of the crossings were smooth, but during a couple trips, six-foot waves sent most of us to the head where we vomited until the boat stopped moving in Nassau or Freeport.

In those days, the boat trips were the only occasions when we saw our father for more than one or two days at a time. When the family was home, he showed up every week or so and stayed only a few nights. I assumed he was busy working or away on a business trip, but I never heard anyone ask him about it.

Life was easy and sweet when Dad wasn't around. Without his criticism and derision looming, we were all free to be ourselves. We all got used to a home life that rarely included him, but we knew whenever a holiday was on the horizon, we'd all be expected to pack and travel to wherever he wanted to go. That usually meant going back to Florida to the *Robert R*, so it was no surprise when, for our spring break in 1975, we all flew to the Ocean Reef Club in Key Largo. All except for Lee. I always asked if she'd go with us, and she always answered that she loved time alone. I'd never met anyone who liked to be alone as much as Lee did.

One evening after dinner, Barb and I sat in the boat's galley booth playing backgammon. Mom was nearby in the master stateroom getting ready for bed, and Dad was watching television two levels up in the saloon. Just after 11:00, the phone rang. We almost never got calls that late, so right away I worried something might have happened to Lee. Several minutes after the phone rang, Mom practically stumbled out of the room, her face drained of color, her arms crossed in front and wrapped around her back. When she entered the galley, her hands were trembling. I'd never seen her like this.

"Mom? Are you okay?"

She remained speechless, staring straight ahead glassy-eyed, as if my sister and I weren't there. Then she ran to the sink and vomited. Now I was really scared. Barb and I looked at each other, then we both jumped up and rushed to her side. I grabbed a towel, and Barb handed Mom a glass of water.

"Are you okay, Mom?" I asked.

"No, I'm not okay."

"Maybe you ate a bad oyster at dinner," I said.

"No, that's not it," she said as she stumbled back to the stateroom.

Shortly afterward, Dad joined her in there, and Barb and I listened as they argued, their heated voices getting louder and louder.

"Who was that woman on the phone?" Mom yelled.

Barb and I clapped our hands over our mouths, communicating with wide eyes. I was thirteen years old, and Barb had just turned fifteen. We were both old enough to know those words meant something was very wrong.

"It's none of your concern!" he yelled back. "Stay out of my damned business, and I'll stay out of yours!"

Barb and I tried to continue our backgammon game, but my stomach was now churning with the burn of acid I experienced whenever something upset me. Barb kept her head down and stared at the game board as if nothing had happened. Our parents fought for about fifteen more minutes, and then they went silent. Barb and I finished our game and didn't talk about what we'd just overheard.

The following morning, I was on deck quietly listening to the water slap against the side of the boat, when Mom came up the stairs and said, "Your father flew back to Chicago. He had last-minute meetings."

I was tired of hearing about Dad's business meetings and business trips. It was always business this and business that with him, his easy out whenever he wanted to leave. "But I thought we were all going to be together all week," I said.

"Not this time."

"Mom, who was that call from late last night? After the call, you and Dad started yelling."

She said, "Sweetheart, it was nothing." Then she went back down to her room.

For the rest of the vacation, Mom spent most of her time in her room. I think she wanted to sleep most of her days away. While she was unavailable, the rest of us took off and explored the Ocean Reef Club and the surrounding areas. We rode around in golf carts, splashed in the pool, played with the beach club's pet dolphins, and took out our little dinghy to go fishing and to explore intercoastal canals. Without Dad, we could do whatever we wanted, including ordering take-out food and attending parties at the Ocean Reef Club. With him out of the picture, our time in Florida felt more like a vacation. But Mom had us all worried. We didn't know if she was sick or missing Dad or what.

Five days after the late-night phone call, we went home where Lee greeted us with a big smile. "I sure missed you! How was your trip?"

Mom didn't answer. She just walked past Lee and into the kitchen. We'd just spent a week in Florida, but her skin was pale.

"Mrs. Krilich, can I get you something to eat or drink?" Lee asked.

"No, thank you," Mom answered in a weak voice. "I'm going to go upstairs to rest, if you don't mind."

Over the next several weeks, Lee had to start cooking more because Mom slept most of the days away. Mom sat with us for meals but barely touched her food, and her clothes were becoming loose and baggy. She stopped putting on makeup, which made her face look really sunken and gaunt. The lack of makeup really shook me. My mother was beautiful, and she almost never even came downstairs without looking put together. On most days, she looked like she was ready for a cocktail party even if she was only going to spend the day at home doing chores.

I knew something was changing in Mom's life when she asked if we could start running together. She'd never shown any interest in exercise, and I didn't understand why she had a sudden interest in fitness. At the time, I was running almost every night after dinner, even if it was dark outside. It gave me peace from our home life. Now Mom wanted to run with me.

We started each outing by walking down the driveway, then turning onto Rainbow Road where we began jogging. Sometimes we jogged for an hour, and when we did, Mom seemed happier, maybe just a bit lighter somehow.

One day during one of our longer runs, we stopped for a break so Mom could catch her breath. I looked up to watch the quarreling birds in the oak trees as dark clouds gathered overhead. There was a storm coming. Mom planted her hands on her hips and in a quivering voice said, "I need to tell you what's happening with your father."

"Is Dad okay?"

"Yes, he's fine. It's me who's not fine. Do you remember the call that came through very late when we were in Key Largo?"

Of course I did. I'd been burning with curiosity ever since that night. What a relief Mom was finally talking about it. Maybe whatever she was about to say would explain why she'd stopped eating. "Of course. And I remember all the fighting."

"That night I picked up the phone at the same time your father did, and he didn't know I was listening. I heard a woman's voice. It was your father's mistress."

"*Mistress?* Dad has a *mistress?*"

"Yes, but there's more. She has a three-year-old son with your father." Mom's voice cracked as she said, "son."

For several seconds, I stood silent. Tears welled in my eyes as I tried to make sense of what I was hearing. How could he do this to Mom, to all of us? Then she hugged me, and we held each other for a while.

I wanted all this ugliness to go away, but I had no idea what I could do about anybody's mess of a marriage, least of all my parents'. For a long time, I'd understood there was something destructive about my father's insatiable hunger for more. I'd always known it had been about having more money and more possessions, but now I knew it included more women and even more children. *Wow*, I thought, *our family's so broken*. It was terribly upsetting news, but at least now some things about my family life made more sense. My father rarely came home because he was living a double life. I had a half brother out there somewhere! What was I supposed to do with that information? Was Dad even going to talk to us kids about it?

Mom was no longer out of breath, and she started jogging in place. Then she stopped and said, "How would you feel if I left your father?"

What a question. And she was asking *me*, her thirteen-year-old. I tried to think fast so I could offer an answer that didn't make me sound like a child. But how *would* I feel? Almost without thinking, I asked, "Are you happy?"

"No. I am *not* happy," Mom said.

I thought, *Now what do I say?* She'd been married twenty-five years, and her marriage was making her miserable. She'd lost way too much weight, and she rarely laughed or even smiled anymore. As I tried to think of what to say next, I gazed all around, down Rainbow Road, up at the darkening sky and the birds. Then I looked straight at my mother. "Mom, you deserve to be happy. You've been good to all of us, and you're the one who keeps the family going. If you're not happy, you shouldn't stay married." It wasn't lost on me that at the age of thirteen, although I'd never so much as kissed a boy, I was offering marital advice.

Mom kept talking as if she was in a conversation with a peer. "Most of all, I'm worried about you kids. I've read horror stories in *Reader's Digest* about children committing suicide or turning to drugs after their parents split up."

"I wouldn't worry about anybody committing suicide, Mom," I said. "And yeah, drugs are all around these days, but we're fine. And we'll be fine with whatever you decide."

She was silent for several seconds, and I wondered if she thought what I'd just offered was silly. But then she said, "And then I think you kids have been through a lot with your father and me and maybe a divorce would let you finish growing up in a peaceful home."

I thought that was a good point. "If you're miserable, you should get out of the marriage, but if you're in love and believe in it, then maybe stay and make it work."

I had no idea what I was talking about. I must have gotten that blather from *The Dating Game* or an episode of *Love, American Style*. I loved watching such adult TV shows. I always thought by watching without my parents knowing about it, I was just getting away with something, but maybe I'd picked up a few things along the way.

Mom and I jogged back home, and when we reached our driveway we stopped, and she said, "Thanks for listening to me and for giving me your thoughts. It helped a lot."

Her words made me feel like a full-blown adult.

Long before my mother picked up the phone in Florida, I knew something was wrong between my parents. Their relationship didn't look anything like those from my favorite shows and movies, *The Brady Bunch*, *Mary Poppins*, and *The Sound of Music*. The men in those stories took pride in their families and were kind to women.

I wondered about Lee's marriage. I imagined it had been a very happy one, and then one day, *poof*, gone in one tragic accident. I wondered if she missed romantic love. Maybe that was why she read so many Harlequin romance novels. She seemed happy being part of our family now, but what must she have felt spending day after week after year with us instead of with the two people she'd planned to be with forever? Instead of living the happy life that was stolen from her, she had to live in the middle of the messed-up marriage that made my mother miserable. How unfair all of it seemed.

Then I thought about what it might mean to be a wife. As nice and sometimes even glamorous as being married looked on TV, the only marriage I'd ever seen up close was the one in my own house. Whenever I was in a room with both of my parents, I felt myself clenching my teeth and sometimes realized I'd made a fist. If somebody else's marriage could make me feel that tense, I wanted nothing to do with it, any of it—not a ring, a wedding, or a husband. Nobody was going to catch me saying, "I do," or God forbid, "Till death do us part," if it meant the kind of fighting and tension that filled the air of our house.

During our next jog together, my mother told me she'd shared everything with Lee. That was a relief. I knew Mom needed an adult to confide in. When Dad wasn't around, Mom and Lee were safe to talk, and I often overheard them talking about my parents' marriage as they sat in the kitchen. It was almost as if our home had become a counseling center dedicated to figuring out how to tolerate my dad while he was still living under the same roof. And it seemed to be a place meant for trying to figure out what Mom should do next.

In the days since my mother had overheard the phone call, whenever my father was home—which wasn't often—the air was thick with tension. It was as if everyone in the house held their breath until he left. One morning after Dad left for work, I sat at the kitchen table eating breakfast. Lee turned to my mother and said, "Mrs. Krilich, you should not tolerate his belittling. It's not acceptable for a man to treat a woman like that."

"I'll try not to take Bob's comments personally," Mom said, "but I keep wondering if I haven't been a good enough wife. What if I didn't do enough to keep him happy?" Mom sighed and massaged her temples.

"Mrs. Krilich, how many times do I have to tell you, you've done *nothing* wrong? You've been nothing but a devoted wife and mother, but *everything* is wrong with how Mr. Krilich treats you." Then she added, "And listen here, there's no shame in seeking a divorce from a man who has committed adultery."

I held my breath waiting to hear my mother's reply.

Mom said, "I never imagined being divorced, but his abuse is crushing me."

It made me a little sick to think of my father doing things that could be called "abuse" and that my mother was feeling crushed.

"Mrs. Krilich, if I may, you have proof he's cheating. A child is undeniable evidence of his infidelity. All you need to do is to stand up for yourself and not fear him. Maybe you should see a counselor. They could help give you strength and get you to take the next steps."

I had no idea how counseling would help Mom; I didn't even know what counselors did for people. But if Lee thought it was a good idea, it had to be a good idea.

Within a week, Mom found a marriage counselor and divorce attorney and started meeting with them every week.

During all this, my father still lived with us, so Mom was stealthy about her appointments. Sometimes when I was doing homework in the kitchen, Dad called from the office looking for Mom, and I heard Lee lie for her, quickly saying, "Mr. Krilich, she's at the grocery store," or "Mr. Krilich, she's at a school function."

I could hear his angry voice from where I sat. "When the hell is she getting home?"

"I'm not sure, but I'll tell her you called."

"How are the meetings going?" Lee asked one morning while she and Mom sat and drank coffee. As was often the case, I sat at the table listening to every word while pretending to be interested in my breakfast or a book.

"The counselor advised me to make the marriage work by continuing counseling, and the attorney advised me to divorce."

"The counselor makes money if you stay, and the lawyer makes money if you divorce."

"Yes," my mother said. "Makes it difficult to know what to do with the advice."

"This is when you should listen to your heart."

Mom's voice brightened. "Get this, my attorney says I have a legal right to fifty percent of Bob's wealth. It never occurred to me I might get a settlement. All this time I've been frozen with fear about how I'd survive after a divorce."

"You deserve fifty percent because you built that company with your husband. It's the law. And you should be careful. I've read that sometimes men hide their assets."

"How can he do that? I know what he owns and most of it is land," Mom said.

"They have their ways. I've read about it. Your lawyer will have to be sharp."

My mother massaged her temples. "This is all so stressful. My doctor thinks I'm headed for a nervous breakdown. I told him I'm having trouble sleeping and am falling behind on my household responsibilities."

"What does he say you should do about it?"

"He recommended I go on antidepressants, but I've never taken anything stronger than aspirin in my life."

"I think you should trust your doctor."

There Lee went again, sounding so wise. Her advice always came so quickly and easily, it was as if she had a library of answers all in order and ready to go.

After months of seeing a therapist and a divorce attorney, my mother was finally ready to serve my father divorce papers. She'd been preparing us kids for some time by asking how we felt about it. None of my siblings seemed particularly upset about the idea of our parents splitting up. I was relieved. Dad was barely around anymore anyway. I didn't know what life would look like as the child of divorced people, but like Mom, I was ready to move on.

$\underset{\text{\tiny{}}}{}$ 9

One beautiful September day in 1975, I rushed out the front door as the early morning sun sent lasers of brilliant light through the apple trees. I flipped up the kickstand on my Schwinn bike, eager to ride to school on this perfect autumn day. Lee came scrambling out the door waving a brown paper bag. "Don't forget your lunch!"

"Thanks, Lee!"

"And be careful riding to school."

"I will," I waved back as I pedaled away.

I'd recently started eighth grade, and five days a week I rode my bike twenty minutes to school, then at the end of the day I rode it home. I usually left the house at 7:25 a.m., which got me to school in plenty of time for the first-class bell at 8:10. But that semester, I'd already been late twice, and a third tardy would mean after-school detention. I wasn't about to stick myself with detention or to let it smear my record.

My first class was math, my favorite subject, and I was excited to get to class early, so I cranked up the speed when I turned onto Rainbow Road from our driveway, zipping out under the canopy of majestic oak and maple trees. I was riding alone but had arranged to meet my friend Mandy partway through the ride. We'd find each other on Lake Zurich Road to ride the rest of the way together.

The first three-quarters of a mile along Rainbow Road was a long stretch of flat asphalt with sharp curves. Drinking in the freedom, I rode for a while with "no hands" but grabbed the handlebars tight as I approached the steep descent toward Cuba Road. I concentrated on staying straight and steady as I approached Cuba Road, the most dangerous part of the ride where cars sped like crazy and whipped up powerful gusts that almost knocked me off my bike.

I waited for a break in the traffic that would allow me to turn right on Cuba Road, then cross to the opposite side to ride against the oncoming traffic. In the distance to my left was a curve, and beyond the curve were railroad tracks. All I had to do right now was cross Cuba Road as fast as I could, then I'd be onto the easy part.

I looked left, then right. The coast was clear, so I turned right fast and started crossing the road while gripping the handlebars and standing on the pedals to give myself power and speed.

That's the last thing I remember.

I woke up to bright lights, the bustling of nurses, and a cacophony of beeps and rings and shuffling, squeaking shoes. My first thought was, *Am I in my bedroom? Am I late?* I couldn't bear to think of missing math class. *Where's Mandy? Did we meet?*

No, this wasn't my room. This place was lit up like a nighttime football stadium. My eyes stung, so I squeezed them tight, and when I opened them again, I realized I was in a hospital bed. I couldn't make sense of anything, so I drifted off to sleep until the sounds of doctors and nurses woke me again. This time I awoke to doctors standing all around me, whispering.

Why was I in a hospital surrounded by doctors? A nurse wearing a blue cap and scrubs approached my bed, leaned in close, and in a voice barely above a whisper asked several ridiculously simple questions. I was foggy-headed and mesmerized by her enormous blue eyes and her skin, which was silkier than any I'd ever seen, but I answered her questions clearly, I thought. "Sandy, I'm thirteen, and today is Friday."

As I spoke, I heard the words struggling to escape my lips, and I started to panic, but not about my state of mind. "I can't be late!" I seemed to both yell and mumble. Oh man, I didn't want detention.

I noticed a clock on the wall. It was already 5:00? I hadn't just missed a class; I'd missed the whole day! Blue Eyes looked at me blankly as I struggled to speak. Why didn't she understand me?

Moments of clarity came and went as if I was drifting in and out of a hazy dream. And each time I resurfaced, the light seemed too bright, all the sounds too loud.

Then I lifted a hand to my face. That's when I felt the bandages. Acid rushed through my stomach as I realized my face was covered in gauze. That explained why my lips felt so funny. I was wrapped so tightly, I could barely move my mouth. I reached up and felt my hair. It was crusty and hardened, and when I brought my hand down in front of my face, I saw it was speckled with dried blood. Then I slid my hand along my forehead and felt more bandages. My entire head was wrapped like a mummy!

Glancing down, I saw along my arms a road map of blood-ied scrapes. My legs were sore, and I guessed they were cut up too, but I couldn't see them under the sheet. Then I dozed off again, and when I woke up, I was both confused and irritated that I couldn't stay awake.

A gray-haired doctor wearing glasses walked into the room, went straight to the foot of the bed, and pinched my right big toe. "Ouch!" I mumble-yelled.

"That's very good," he said. Then he pinched my left big toe.

"Ouch!"

He asked me to lift my right leg, then my left. What was with this guy? I was a middle school athlete—of course I could lift my legs.

He jotted some things on his clipboard, then he said, "I hope you know it's a miracle you have full movement in your body. It's a miracle you're here at all."

I felt another surge of acid in my stomach.

"You've been in a very serious accident. A car hit you this morning while you were riding your bike to school."

I couldn't remember any car accident. I asked, "Am I alright? Am I going to be okay?" It was all garble.

Just beyond the doctor, I saw my mom entering the room wiping her nose with a fistful of tissues. Lee walked in behind her, wearing her favorite Cubs sweatshirt. They both stood by my bed and gripped the rail. I could tell they were both fighting back tears.

"Sandy, I'm here," Mom said with a trembling voice.

Lee forced a smile. "Hi, sweetheart, you're going to be okay." Lee being there told me how serious my situation was.

She rarely left the property on Rainbow Road unless it was for a Cubs game. Both their faces contorted in pain, and the sight of them standing there in anguish started my tears flowing down my bandages. My thoughts were a tangle of confusion and fear, but having them both there also comforted me. I knew that however bad it was, those two would be by my side.

For a while, nobody spoke. We three just cried.

It would be a month before I understood what had happened to me. According to the story Robin and Barb told, while they were driving to their school, they saw several cars stopped on the side of Cuba Road. When they slowed down, they saw paramedics working on someone laid out on the ground.

"Slow down! Isn't that Sandy's bike?" Robin screamed to Barb.

"Oh my God, yes," Barb answered.

Barb pulled the car to the side of the road, then Robin leapt out and ran toward the paramedic while Barb made a U-turn and raced back to find my parents.

The paramedic gave Robin instructions to keep talking to me to try to keep me awake. Robin said she repeated, "Everything is going to be alright," again and again. "You were shaking like crazy," she said. "And there was blood everywhere. But what freaked me out was that your eyes were rolling backward. The paramedic told me to just keep talking to you to keep you from slipping into a coma."

I remembered none of this.

Meanwhile, back at the house, my parents were both still in bed when Barb rushed into their room and shouted, "Sandy's been hit by a car!"

My parents jumped out of bed and started pulling on clothes. Then my father ran out of the bedroom calling behind him, "I'll call you as soon as I can. Don't go down there until I find out what's going on."

While he was racing to the accident, my mother called Lee to join her in prayer in her bedroom. Twenty minutes later, while they were still kneeling in prayer, my father called and told my terrified mother, "Sandy's lost a lot of blood, and the paramedic says she has a less than fifty percent chance of surviving. Her blood pressure has dropped to a dangerous level. You need to meet us at Northwestern Hospital right away."

A well-known plastic surgeon named Dr. Schwartz became my primary physician following the accident, and for the next five years, I underwent several surgeries to remove shards of glass and rock that had embedded deep within my scars. Dr. Schwartz also worked to restore symmetry to my face. There was a deep cut from the top of my forehead down to the space between my eyebrows, and under my right eye was a big upside-down L-shaped mark that had been cut into my skin by windshield glass. It had missed my eye by a millimeter. Another piece of glass had torn my upper cheek from my lower cheek, leaving part of my face detached. Yet another piece of glass had sliced my upper lip in half.

After three weeks in the hospital, I still felt pain in my legs, arms, and pelvis, and I had constant headaches, but I was sent home and told to get a lot of rest but also to keep moving—just not to do anything strenuous. So I spent hours wandering our property, inside and out, singing softly to myself while I pulled weeds or watched squirrels prance around the yard. When the trees lost their leaves, I raked them into piles. I wasn't allowed to lift anything, so I couldn't carry them to the dumpster. But I raked and raked. The motion of it was soothing, and I was utterly grateful to be outdoors and nowhere near a hospital.

I wasn't depressed; I just felt lost and often detached from myself. There was a spaciness to my waking hours I didn't understand. Though my body began to heal, my mind still felt wounded. I wasn't quick with thoughts or words anymore. Past events like my birthdays were a blur, and it scared me. I couldn't get a grip on who I was now, so I was left feeling disconnected from most things that had once been familiar or important to me.

After a month of healing, my doctor decided it was time for me to go back to school. I was scared to face my friends with my hacked-up face because I was sure they'd think I was a monster. I thought I should get a haircut that would cover as much of my face as possible, but I knew it was of no use. My face was ruined now, and people were going to find me repulsive. My only escape from feeling awkward came when I was with Mandy. She acted cool about it all, just pretending nothing had happened.

I walked into math class on my first day back, dressed in loose-fitting clothes that hung on me like pajamas. As I settled into my usual desk near the front of the room, most of the other students looked away.

"Welcome back, Sandy," my favorite math teacher said.

As my teacher went through the day's lesson, I felt lost. Though math had been the subject I'd always felt most competent in, now I had no idea what was going on. And if it wasn't bad enough that I was now clueless in my best subject, my first day back to school was picture day. Having a photo snapped of me with a road map of scars on my face and holes in my forehead was going to be devastating. I dashed to a pay phone and called home.

"Mom, can you give me permission to skip the photo session today? These pictures are going in the yearbook!"

"Have them take your photos, but we won't buy them. Don't worry about the yearbook. Nobody looks back at those pictures anyway."

Nobody looked at yearbook pictures? At the end of the year, *everybody* looked at yearbook pictures! But I didn't have the energy for a battle, so I did as I was told.

From behind the camera, the chirpy photographer said, "Give me your best smile." I stayed quiet. I didn't have a best smile, a worst smile, or any smile. The right side of my face and my lip were still stitched up. How was I supposed to smile with a stitched lip? Nothing about me that day was my best, and it was all going to be immortalized in the yearbook.

At home, Mom and Lee continued to shower me with words of encouragement.

"Sandy," Mom often said brightly, "you are so brave and beautiful. And you're a survivor. You're a miracle!"

But the mirror told a different story. My face was a field of red and white bumps, and my scars remained dark red. My eyes looked dull, and my once full, plump lips were now uneven, thanks to a scar that now ran through my upper lip where glass had sliced it right through to the other side. What I hated most was my asymmetrical face. I was crooked now.

My mother was beauty conscious, so she had a lot of empathy for me. One day she handed me a bottle of vitamin E pills and said, "Poke one of these pills with a pin, then squeeze the oil on your scars before bedtime. I read in *Reader's Digest* vitamin E helps scars heal faster."

I gave it a try for a couple of days but then quit because the oil smelled like rotten fish.

With each surgery, I hoped for a miracle, that I'd wake up normal again, my face perfectly symmetrical, my skin like creamy silk, and not a scar on my face. But the improvements brought about by each surgery were marginal at best. During each procedure, the doctor removed more dirt and pebbles from my face, but then he'd re-stitch the scar again, and I'd have to start the healing process all over.

I was a brand-new teenager, so while on the outside I started breaking out with acne, inside I was a constant churn of anxiety and self-consciousness made worse by the fact that I couldn't focus or remember even the simplest things. Two months after the accident, I still couldn't follow my family's conversations or the dialogue in movies. I couldn't engage in a meaningful conversation because my thoughts bounced all around and I spun away from the subject we'd started with. I realized I was better off not saying anything because when I spoke, people looked at me with confusion and pity.

The doctors confirmed the concussion had caused nerve damage, particularly affecting the left side of my cerebrum, which controls speech. The band of nerves connecting my brain's two hemispheres sustained severe injuries, which is why my memories of events before the accident were hazy and elusive. I'd remember an event with a relative but not where or when the event occurred. I'd be able to recall a family trip but only in general, without details, as if I hadn't been there but someone had told me about it.

The doctors said there was nothing they could do to fix the nerve damage. I just had to let time pass and hope it healed. That wasn't good enough for Lee. "Let's get you writing in a journal," she said one Saturday afternoon.

"I tried that. I didn't have anything to write about."

"Start by writing about your day. What time you woke up, what you wore, where you went, and whether you met anyone new. Then think about how your day felt, whether it was fun or a struggle, whether you felt sad or if someone disappointed you."

"Okay," I said. But I expected I'd quit by day two.

Every night before bedtime, I sat on my bed and wrote something like, *Dear Diary, today I woke up at 7:15 a.m.* After about thirty days of logging my wake-up time and what I wore, I lost interest. I didn't want to disappoint Lee, but I admitted to her I'd stopped writing in the journal.

She said, "Sweetheart, writing your feelings down will help you reconnect with who you are in all this confusion, just keep trying. It takes time."

So I kept writing in my journal, but I couldn't process my feelings. I felt numb, and I didn't have words to describe the emptiness.

One day Lee saw me struggling to answer questions about a chapter I'd just read for history class. She picked up my textbook and skimmed the chapter I'd been trying to focus on. "No wonder," she said. "History was never my best subject either. To become a good reader, you need to read books you're interested in."

"I'm sure not interested in the Renaissance period!"

"How about I show you a few of my books, and you can pick one out? If your mother approves, you can read it for entertainment. One of my favorite books is *The Other Side of Midnight*, by Sidney Sheldon."

Mom said yes, and I started to read the book for about thirty minutes a day. The story was full of treachery and twists, and I found myself completely confused as well as completely frustrated because I knew months earlier that book would have been no problem for me. Even reading a teen magazine frustrated me as I struggled to grasp the essence of the articles.

I knew something was very wrong, but I was determined not to give in to the possibility that I was now feebleminded. I had to figure out how to get smarter, how to pronounce words correctly, and how to comprehend what I read.

My local community center was offering a speed-reading class. The sign advertised that the program would increase comprehension and reading speed by teaching people to skim pages while still taking in the meaning. It said students would create a magical paintbrush by visualizing the story. I couldn't sign up fast enough.

The class was hard for me, but every day I practiced the skills I was taught. And it worked. I started to read with more understanding and confidence, and after a few weeks, I asked Lee if I could read another one of her books. She suggested another Sidney Sheldon book called *Master of the Game*, and after Mom approved, I started reading it and didn't want to put it down for meals or to go to sleep. After I finished the book, Lee gave me another and then another. I started to like reading again, and that gave me a boost of optimism I desperately needed after the accident.

While I was beginning to feel more confident about my mind, physically I was nowhere near my old self. Since the accident, I'd been clumsy and awkward. While feeding the dogs one evening, I tripped over the track of the sliding glass door, and dog food went flying everywhere. One night Mom made a spaghetti dinner, and while I was serving everyone, a plate slipped out of my hand, scattering spaghetti across the floor. On another occasion, I made a bowl of popcorn for Dad, and while carrying it to him in the family room, I stumbled on the carpet, and buttery kernels flew everywhere. These incidents were happening more and more, and Lee was always watching, always trying to help me feel better about whatever I was dealing with. She helped me clean up the messes and whispered guidance like, "Sweetheart, you're moving around too quickly. You need to slow down and watch what you're doing." I tried to do as she suggested, but I was haunted by the reality that the new me was worse than the old one in every way.

But Lee didn't give up. She started making lists for me, writing out my chores for the day, and putting the lists in my hand. She talked to me about what I was going through, how I felt about the changes and my new limitations. While the members of my family seemed focused on the external aspects of my accident—fascinated I'd crashed through the windshield of a car that was going over eighty miles an hour and lived—Lee paid attention to what was going on inside me.

I'd suffered a severe concussion and a traumatic brain injury, but nobody in my household ever talked about it. I was never even taken to a neurologist or brain surgeon for an assessment. My family focused on the external scars. They seemed interested only in how my face was healing and whether I'd get my balance back. They watched to see if I was starting to walk normally again. But Lee made herself *part* of my healing and helped with both my external and internal recovery. She was tireless. And it was during this time she asked me to help her work on puzzles.

I'd always thought putting together jigsaw puzzles was a simple thing. It was something I'd always associated with little kids and old people. It was just a way to kill time. But I was about to learn how puzzles could mean so much more.

10

Lee and I did our first puzzle together shortly after I returned home following my accident. It was a three-thousand-piece project, and its subject was a majestic, snowy-peaked mountain range in Switzerland that looked like a scene from *The Sound of Music*. When Lee laid all the pieces out, I thought, *How on earth are we going to be able to put that puzzle together in this lifetime?* But for Lee, puzzling wasn't about a goal. It wasn't a race. Nothing was measured or rewarded. It was a quiet activity with a kind of meditative quality that for her seemed to offer deep satisfaction. And in no time, I began to understand that satisfaction.

Whenever Lee and I had a puzzle in progress sprawled across the big marble coffee table in the living room, I couldn't wait for school to end so I could get home and back to puzzling with her. When the bus stopped in front of our house, I jumped off and sprinted up the driveway and into the living room where Lee sat on the white leather couch that stretched across the length of the back wall. Every afternoon she settled in this quiet corner of the house, her head bent down as she focused on all those scattered pieces, hundreds of curved and angled pieces of the puzzle.

When Lee worked on a jigsaw puzzle, she did it with a kind of quiet reverence, and when I watched her, I developed great admiration for her gentle calm. Her graceful movements were beautiful to me, and I envied the peace she seemed to experience. The process of working on a puzzle often meant long periods with no conversation and no physical exercise. The activity called for the opposite of the wound-up kind of energy I was usually churning. Lee seemed to know it was the kind of pursuit I needed to calm my anxiety and soothe my brain after the accident.

When Lee first took the Switzerland puzzle out of the box, she turned each piece face up and meticulously sorted them into little batches based on color, size, and shape. It was mesmerizing to watch the delicate movements of her bent fingers as they worked with what looked to me like an overwhelming number of puzzle elements.

"Your pile is over here." She pointed and gently slid a mound of puzzle pieces closer to my side of the coffee table. I stared at the pile, already overwhelmed by how many elements were involved in this exercise. Lee seemed to read my mind. She smiled and said, "Just focus on one piece at a time."

As I watched and sorted, I noticed the logic of Lee's system. After she sorted all the pieces, she separated the straight-edged pieces from the middle ones. This step was the beginning of establishing the boundaries of the picture. Once the groups were divided, she began to assemble the puzzle's outer frame. For a puzzle that size, creating the outer border could sometimes take a week or more. She patiently held up piece after piece, comparing its color to the picture on the box and its color and shape to the pieces already snapped into place. After the frame of the puzzle was finished, she sat back and sighed with relief. Completing the framework was the most manageable step, the most orderly. The remaining pieces represented countless options and combinations, so to me it seemed that after the outline was created, the real work began. Sometimes we talked as we filled in the body of the puzzle, but sometimes we worked for long stretches without saying anything. I liked it both ways. When we did speak, we talked about the Cubs spring training, who the new players were, and who had retired. We talked about new books Lee recommended and what was coming up in the *TV Guide* that she was looking forward to watching. One afternoon, when we were about a quarter of the way through the puzzle, I asked her why she'd never gotten her driver's license and had never flown on an airplane.

"I was never interested."

"But you seem to love to learn about new places, different countries. And you seem to love the beautiful scenery."

"I sure do, but I can travel right here at home through my books and puzzles. Just think of all the money and hassle I save." She chuckled. "I like staying home, and I especially like being alone," she said.

"But it would be so nice to go somewhere with you someday," I said.

"Maybe someday."

I knew to leave it there.

Lee had a subtle way of offering guidance when she wanted me to figure something out on my own, and the quietness of puzzling allowed me to observe this skill in action. When she saw me fishing around for a puzzle piece or trying to force a snap between two pieces that looked alike, she slid a piece across the table toward me and said something like, "Maybe this piece goes in the corner you're working on." And with that, I'd happily put down the troubling piece and switch my focus to the one Lee had handed me.

"Sometimes you just need to put a piece down and deal with it again later," she said. "And when you come back to it, you sometimes find that something in your mind clicks, and you see things differently. With each piece, you're solving a problem, but it takes patience and perseverance. When you get stuck, don't give up. Just move on to something else, and go back to the tough part later with fresh eyes."

After three months of working on the Swiss Alps puzzle, Lee and I were nearly finished. It was mid-January, and we'd worked on it throughout the holiday break. Now all of us kids were back in school, and as usual, I couldn't wait to get home to work on the puzzle with Lee. We were down to what appeared to be about fifty pieces left. Lee said this was a really exciting time during puzzle work. "It starts to go really fast at this point."

When there were about ten pieces left, I heard Caesar, our Old English sheepdog, outside yapping with excitement because someone had pulled into the driveway. When the front door opened, he bolted into the living room and took a soaring leap right onto the middle of the coffee table. I watched the scene as if in slow motion: Caesar landed on the table, the puzzle split into big sections that slid in all directions, and hundreds of little puzzle pieces flew onto the floor and couch and behind pillows. Some of the puzzle that had broken off in sheets slid off the table, flipped over, and broke apart into even smaller chunks, like pieces of honeycomb broken from a bee's hive.

Lee gasped and clapped her hand over her mouth. Then she pressed both hands to her face and moaned, "Oh no. Oh my God."

I jumped to my feet, grabbed Caesar by the collar, and shouted, "Bad dog! Get outside!" and yanked him to the back door.

When I was back in the living room, my stomach ached for Lee. Months of work, all the care and precision and joy—all of it lay scattered on the floor like shards of broken glass. She turned away from me as if she was embarrassed over how emotional she'd been. That's when I realized it was much more than a puzzle to Lee. I sat down and wrapped my arms around her. It was the kind of tight embrace she gave me when I fell and skinned my knee or when my dad hurt my feelings.

Gradually, Lee regained her composure. She took a few deep breaths and began to collect the strewn puzzle pieces and place them back on the marble coffee table. The warm, adoring gaze I knew so well began to return to her eyes, and that calmed me.

As I helped her collect the puzzle pieces and place them back on the coffee table, I thought about how much lay beneath surfaces, how much other people couldn't see. It was like my parents' marriage: to other people, our family life probably looked shiny and happy. That house! That land! Those beautiful kids! But just one look a little deeper would reveal that nothing was as it appeared. I wondered which aspects of Lee weren't as they appeared. Who was she, really? How did she know so much about how to deal with abusive men? When so many people in my life were clueless about the depths and ramifications of my traumatic brain injury, why did Lee seem to have such a natural understanding of it all? And why did she have dentures at such a young age? What kind of youth would have included such awful dental care that she'd have lost all her teeth? Why did she walk so strangely, as if she'd been born with one leg shorter than the other? Why did she dread bathtubs? Where had her obsession with baseball begun? Why did she constantly immerse herself in crossword puzzles, jigsaw puzzles, dictionaries, Scrabble, movies, and books? What was her life like before she came into our family? And *why* wouldn't she talk about any of it?

One day after school the following spring, Lee unpacked the new puzzle she'd let me choose, a 3,500-piece Paris boulangerie scene depicting shelves and carts and display cases full of Parisian delights, including croissants, baguettes, madeleines, *pain au chocolat*, and other beautiful pastries. It was a brightly colored, visual feast. At the time, I was taking a French class, so I was fascinated by anything having to do with Paris.

"Wow, this puzzle is massive," I said, helping her begin to sort the pieces. "How will we ever finish it?"

She smiled. "We'll find our way there."

It didn't take long to see our usual table was too small for this enormous project, so Lee said, "We need to create a bigger workspace. Let's see what we can find in the garage."

In no time we found a big piece of plywood, bigger than the coffee table, and transferred the puzzle to our new, mobile puzzle platform. It was perfect. And it calmed my ever-present anxiety that we might have another diving dog incident. Now if we heard an animal charging our way, we could just elevate the entire project out of danger.

It took almost four days to snap the outer pieces together. Then we spent at least a couple hours every day for the next eight weeks in our usual routine of sitting across from each other, working in sections, talking and not talking. Thanks to our process, I was often in a state of complete contentment.

Then came that exciting moment when there was only one piece left. Lee held it out to me. "You do the honors."

"Really? *Me*?" It was as if someone had just told me I'd be the one to cut the ribbon at the newest addition to Disney World.

She nodded and smiled. I snapped the piece into place with a click, and we sat there in silence admiring our accomplishment. The puzzle was glorious. A perfect, shiny snapshot of an exotic, delicious scene bursting with vibrant colors and situated in what I thought must be the most exciting place in the world. After a few minutes of admiring the finished puzzle, Lee said, "Sweetheart, can you help me disassemble the puzzle and put it back in the box?"

Put it back in the box? I couldn't fathom the idea of taking it all apart after all the work we'd done for so many months. I gasped. "After all that? Why put it away so soon?"

"Sweetheart, the joy is in the making," she said.

I didn't understand why the joy couldn't be in the making *and* the finishing *and* the keeping. I asked, "Why not leave it here awhile so we can admire it?"

"Because it's the process of doing the puzzle that enriches the soul."

"But I want to hang it on my wall. Maybe we can find someone who frames puzzles."

Lee paused, then said, "That sounds like a lovely idea."

"I'll start calling around right away."

I couldn't wait to show Mom the final product, and I was thrilled at the idea of preserving the enormous project forever, this thing Lee and I created together.

I searched the Yellow Pages until I found Eddie's Fast Frames, a company willing to frame a completed jigsaw puzzle. They said they hadn't done anything like it but would be willing to give it a shot. Now I felt as if I'd come up with an innovative idea, and that thrilled me even more.

After Mom and I returned home from dropping off the puzzle at the frame shop, Lee greeted us at the front door. "I'm so happy you're home," she said. "I think I have a great idea."

"What's that?" I asked.

"I'd like to surprise each of the other kids for Christmas with a framed puzzle of their choice. They can pick the puzzle they like most, and after I put it together, I'll frame it as their Christmas present. Can you keep a secret?"

"I can! And I love that plan." Now I felt even cooler about my puzzle framing idea.

Lee said, "I can finally give every one of you kids a gift that will help you remember me after I'm long gone."

Lee gone. Just hearing those words hit me like a slap. The idea of our life without Lee in it was just too much for me to grasp.

~~~~ 11

A year after my accident, Mom was driving me to a doctor's appointment when it occurred to me I'd almost forgotten about the divorce papers.

I turned to face her. "Mom, I thought you were going to divorce Dad. Wait, wasn't it the day of my accident that you were planning to serve him the divorce papers?"

She scrunched her face up and shook her head. Now I was confused. Why didn't she have a fast answer? Had my mother changed her mind? Was she going to *stay with him*? I suspected her Catholic upbringing had gotten to her.

As I watched my mother struggle to find an answer, I thought about how weird it was that my family never talked about Dad's betrayal. None of us kids, not even my outspoken sister, Robin, talked about it. And Mom and Dad just went about their lives as they had for years. Dad threw himself into his work at the office, and when he was home, he worked on projects around the property. As for the baby half brother out there in the world, we didn't know anything about him, where he lived, who was raising him, whether Dad ever saw him—nothing.

Finally, Mom answered. "Oh, honey, I prayed and told God that if you survived the accident, I'd give your father another chance."

I couldn't believe what I was hearing. "*No!* You made a deal with God?"

"I did. And your father wants to make things right." Then she bit her lip.

"How does *that* work? Does he just say, 'abracadabra'— and poof, the child no longer exists?"

At the mention of my father's child with another woman, she winced. "No, that's not how it works. Your father agreed to end the relationship with *her* and provide financial support for the child. That little boy is a child of God, just like the rest of us, and Bob should take financial responsibility."

"You just forgive him, and everything goes on like it never happened?"

"I agreed to forgive your father and give him another chance at our marriage. We built something together, and I don't want to be too quick to throw it away. I'm not saying it's going to be easy to trust him again. It won't be and . . ."

Her voice trailed off, and I realized if I started unloading all my angry thoughts about my disappointing father I'd only make her life worse. So I said, "You're really strong, Mom." Did I mean it? I don't know, but it seemed like a good thing to say. And right away her face brightened.

"Your father booked us on the QE2 to Europe next month. He suggested this two-week voyage for us to celebrate our renewed union."

"That sounds nice," I said.

It sounded awful. Ever since the infamous phone call we all knew Dad had been showering Mom with trips and gifts. That's how he operated. He bought whatever he wanted.

In November 1976, Mom and Dad left on a two-week cruise from New York to London. It was the final trans-Atlantic crossing of the QE2, a one-way trip to England, carrying more than 1,400 passengers. My parents were on the ship for a week and spent the rest of the time in London and Paris. When they returned two weeks later, they were tanned and looked relaxed. That night, during a family dinner, they told us about the trip.

"The trip was nice," Mom said in a flat voice as she gazed out the kitchen window.

Dad was a lot more animated. "We sailed to London and were lucky to have beautiful weather. We spent a day in London, then flew to Paris for a day, then caught our flight home."

I couldn't tell if the clipped storytelling meant there were lots of great stories they couldn't share with kids or that the trip had been a bust. But nobody asked questions, including Lee.

The next morning, as Mom headed out to the car to go grocery shopping, I asked, "Can I come with you?"

"No, honey," she said, "I need to focus on the menus for the week."

About an hour later, she returned home and called out, "Sandy! Can you help me bring the groceries inside?"

I carried groceries into the kitchen and noticed the blank look on my mother's tanned face. As she unpacked the bags, her eyes seemed to be tinged with sadness.

"Mom, is everything okay?"

"I'm fine," she said. "I'm just tired."

But I knew what was going on. Dad had taken her away on a fancy trip to try to win her back, and it hadn't worked. He was a cheater with an illegitimate child, and two weeks of glamorous travel wasn't going to fix any of it. I could tell from the look on my mother's sad face their marriage was over.

Dad, on the other hand, seemed to have hit some magical reset button. One day shortly after their trip, he strolled into the house after work wearing a big smile. His voice boomed as he called out for my mother.

"I have something special for you, Lillian!"

We were all in the kitchen helping set the table for dinner. Mom was busy behind the stove, and Lee was working at the sink while Robin, Barb, and I scurried around grabbing plates, napkins, silverware, and glasses. Dad slithered over to Mom and handed her a neatly wrapped box from Goldin Jewelers. And from behind his back, he pulled out a bouquet of red roses.

"Oh, what a surprise! Thank you, Bob." She forced a smile.

My father was a master at using gifts and money to fix problems, but I could see my mother couldn't be bought.

For the next several months, I watched my parents' marriage dissolve. Dad started taking more business trips, and when he was home, their fighting escalated into screaming matches.

But the deterioration of my parents' marriage wasn't the only troubling event going on under our roof. As Dad descended further into denial and Mom into sadness, my siblings and I were also falling apart. One sister experimented with LSD and landed in the emergency room. Another started shoplifting. Another sibling started selling drugs. And I fell into the grip of an eating disorder. I had become bulimic.

Lee witnessed it all like an eagle watching from above, and she tried to help each of us without pushing too hard. She often waited for a quiet moment and then took one of us aside and asked, "How are you? Tell me how your life has been lately." And she listened. But there didn't seem to be much she could do. We were all barreling toward self-destruction to escape the deterioration of our family life.

My bulimia started shortly after my accident, but for many years before that I'd been gripped by an overwhelming sense of inadequacy. And while living in the haze of my dysfunctional family, I'd never had a clear sense of what was real. We took extravagant vacations, but at home, we lived frugally. We rarely got new clothes for school, and with the exception of when we did chores for Lee, we were never given an allowance, not even for doing yardwork until our fingers bled. My father kept a tight grip on all the family finances, and at home it seemed we were always on the edge of financial ruin, which explained why we were never allowed to take long showers, turn the heat up high in winter, or even use too much toothpaste.

In the mirror, I saw myself getting smaller, weaker, less interesting—just less in every way. I knew I wasn't smart enough or pretty enough to make my intelligent, successful, handsome father proud. I didn't think I was good enough for my family in general, people who in my eyes were a pack of capable, talented, great-looking superstars. As far as I was concerned, my horrible accident had turned a mediocre kid into a family embarrassment.

The bulimia started one day when I was hanging out with my friend Suzy, a girl obsessed with losing weight. "Try a couple of these," she said, shaking a bottle of diet pills at me. "They keep you thin as a model!"

I didn't need to lose weight, but I didn't want her to think I wasn't cool, so I tossed a couple of the pills to the back of my throat and washed them down with a big slug of Tab, my favorite diet cola. Right away, I started buzzing with alert energy and wanted to go outside and run, so we did. Suzy and I must have run five or six miles. After the run we both had as much energy as we'd had before it. And I wasn't hungry at all. I thought those pill were magical.

One weekend night when Suzy stayed at our house for a sleepover, she and I made a huge chocolate cake and ate it all by ourselves. We didn't mind the calories—we figured the diet pills would keep us from getting fat. But after stuffing ourselves with all the cake, we were both nauseated, so Suzy snuck off to the restroom and stuck her fingers down her throat and threw up. When she came out of the bathroom, Suzy told me what she'd done, and I went into the bathroom and tried to copy what she'd described. I made myself gag until I vomited, then gargled with mouthwash. Afterward, we both said what we'd done was gross, but secretly I felt empowered. Being able to control something about my body was an entirely new sensation. That night, Suzy and I agreed we'd never do that disgusting thing again. But I kept it up. Whenever I stuffed myself with all the ice cream and cookies I wanted, which always left me feeling nauseated and fat, I threw it all up and felt slim again.

As usual, Lee had been paying attention. One day while I was in the kitchen helping her with the dishes, she asked, "Sandy, how can you eat so much and stay so thin?"

"I'm always running."

"Yes, I know that. But you've been a runner for a long time. Something's different recently. Your portions are huge, and you're still the skinniest one in the family. It doesn't make sense."

She was onto me! I had to think fast. "Running, swimming, all my chores, all my homework . . . I need the calories to keep going."

Her expression seemed to convey both skepticism and kindness. "Well, sweetheart, if you ever want to talk to me about anything, I'm here. I'll always help you in any way I can, but you need to be honest with me, okay?"

"Okay, that's fair," I said, cringing inside.

I spent the rest of the evening worrying. Would she tell Mom? Should I keep lying to her? I didn't know how to stop the cycle, but I was way too embarrassed to admit that at least twice a day I made myself vomit.

One evening the family—except for Dad—were all gathered for a dinner of roasted chicken, potatoes, vegetables, and bread. Lee sat next to me. After I stuffed myself, I asked my mother, "May I be excused? I need to use the restroom."

"Yes, you may be excused."

I could feel Lee's eyes on me as I walked away from the table.

When I returned, Lee's and my eyes locked. Though I tried not to, I cleared my throat a few times. I didn't want to give her any more clues about what I was up to, but as we all said, Lee had eyes behind her head. She even knew my father was cheating on my mother long before Mom found out. After dinner that night, Lee came up to my room where I was at my desk doing homework. She sat on the edge of my bed. "Sandy, can I ask you something?"

That seemed odd. Lee never asked permission to ask questions. "Sure," I said, trying to sound nonchalant.

She patted the bed next to her, and I got up from my desk and sat by her side. "Are you not feeling well?" she asked.

I knew I was busted. "I'm fine. Why?"

"I noticed chicken floating in the powder room toilet after dinner. Are you having trouble keeping your food down?"

I could feel my face flush with shame. I hated lying to Lee, but I wasn't about to face the humiliation of admitting I voluntarily stuck my finger down my throat every day.

"I don't know what you mean. Chicken in the toilet?"

She stroked my back and whispered in my ear, "It'll be fine. We just need to know if you're okay. You can talk to me anytime."

We? Was she standing in for my mother? Of course, she was. She was doing motherly duties to take the burden from my poor broken mother who was practically drowning in grief. My mother's grief—that was another reason I wouldn't come clean about the bulimia. I couldn't be the problem that tipped my mother over the edge.

"Thanks, Lee, for caring about me. I'll let you know if I ever need help," I said.

Lee left my room and I sighed with relief.

That night, the stress of being confronted by Lee made me want to eat. I waited until I heard her go down to her bedroom, then tiptoed to the kitchen to eat some of my mother's delicious cherry pie. It was so good I ate every bit of the half pie that had been left after dinner. Then I went back up to my room and vomited it all up.

The next morning, as I sat in the kitchen eating breakfast, Lee talked to my mother about me as if I wasn't even sitting there.

"Sandy finished off the pie last night. She has the appetite of a horse. I don't understand how she can eat like that and stay skinny as a string bean."

My mother answered, "When Sandy was in third grade, she was so underweight the school insisted I take her for a doctor's exam. Her pediatrician said she has an unusually high metabolism."

Lee backed off. She knew Mom was too fragile to handle the truth. So for now, my secret was still secret enough.

$\approx$ **12**

From 1976 to 1980, Mom and Dad remained married but seemed to live separate lives. They were polite to each other around the house and slept in the same bed, but it was obvious there was almost nothing left between them. During those years, Mom had been getting stronger, partly thanks to Lee, who had helped my mother realize she deserved better. I often overheard their conversations, the two of them talking like old friends. Again and again, Lee said, "You deserve to be treated with respect." "You deserve an honest man who loves you." "You've done nothing wrong."

Dad continued his rants and insults, but now whenever he railed, Mom just walked out of the room.

By 1980, the only kids living at home were Rob and me. Roseann and Robin were married, Debbie had moved to California, and Barb was in college. Rob and I were worn out by all the tension in our house, and now and then we talked about how much we looked forward to leaving our house forever.

Dad wouldn't move out, and Mom couldn't afford a place that would accommodate her, Lee, Rob, and me, so my parents remained under the same roof for the entire five years of the divorce proceedings. More than once, I overheard Mom tell Lee my father was turning her life into a living hell. What made it all even worse was Dad and his lawyer did whatever they could to drag out the process as long as possible to make Mom drop the divorce. But Lee kept telling her, "Mrs. Krilich, stay strong. Don't let his games get to you. He's trying to manipulate you by making your life miserable. Stick to your plan."

A few weeks after Dad's fiftieth birthday, Mom had him served with divorce papers, but still, he didn't move out. He often came home drunk and angry, stumbling and screaming, but he wouldn't leave.

One morning about three months after Dad's birthday, Mom and Dad were both at the breakfast table. Lee was sitting at Mom's desk, and Rob and I were finishing our eggs when Dad asked me, "Will you be graduating soon?"

"I graduated in December, Dad."

He showed not even a flicker of shame for not already knowing that, but then again, it was understandable he didn't know. At that point, I'd graduated only "on paper." I was planning to walk with my classmates in June to receive my diploma, and until then I'd work, for the experience and the much-needed money.

"What are your plans?"

"I'm starting at Arizona State this fall. Until then, I'll keep working at Household Finance Corporation as an accounting clerk."

The room was graveyard quiet.

I'd always expected my father would pay for my higher education, as he'd paid for my sisters to attend college. His business was flourishing and afforded him luxuries most could only dream of, so I'd never even considered whether he'd pay my way. The ticks on the clock grew louder as I waited for my dad's response. He shifted in his chair, and his brows furrowed.

"You're not going to college. It's a waste of time and money."

By now I knew my father didn't think much of me, especially since the accident, but this was a twist I hadn't seen coming. "What? Why? You sent Roseann, Debbie, and Barb to college, and now you change your mind when it comes to me?"

"You're only going to get married and have babies. You don't need an education for that."

"How do you know what I'm going to do?"

He ignored the question and offered a couple gems of his own. "Why should I invest my hard-earned money in sending *you* to college? How is giving you a college education going to benefit me?"

His words left me speechless, and I felt my shoulders slump.

Just then, Lee got up from the desk and shuffled to the coffee machine near my dad to prepare a fresh pot. I could see from her pinched expression she wasn't going to let this one go.

"Mr. Krilich, your daughter is a bright young lady who will thrive with a college education. Please don't deny her that opportunity. She's worked tirelessly for years to get ready for college."

My mother dropped her fork on the Formica table, and the clatter caused Dad to turn his attention to her. "Bob," she said, "Lee is right. Sandy should go to college." We all waited for my father to say something, anything. But he just sat there and sipped his coffee, looking into the cup as if it were a crystal ball.

My mother continued, her voice trembling, "She's very good at math. Her skills are above average. If she goes to college, she could pursue a business career."

I straightened up in my chair, feeling a surge of confidence. "I *am* going to college. I'm going to get an education and build a career for myself. And *if* I find the right person, *maybe* I'll get married and have a family, but it won't be because I have to depend on a man to support me!"

Mom and Lee looked at each other wide-eyed, and I saw a tiny smile form on my mother's face. The only sound in the kitchen was the ticking of the clock.

My father's hands shook as he picked up the newspaper and for the next few minutes silently turned pages. Then he set the paper down on the table and turned to me.

"Okay. Go to college. But here's the deal: the minute you bring home a report card with less than straight A's, that's the end of it. You're done. I won't shell out another penny for you."

"Fine. I'll get all A's."

While I was away at school, I talked to Mom every Sunday, and if Lee was in the room, Mom handed her the phone. They talked about the situation with Dad—strained and weird—then they told me about Rob, my sisters, the dogs, and whatever other news they had. I worked harder in those first college classes than I'd ever worked on anything, taking extra notes, reading chapters two and three times, and staying up late night after night to study.

When my freshman year ended, Mom met me at the airport and wrapped me in a tight hug. As we drove home, she shared details of the divorce that appeared to have no end in sight. My father fought every proceeding and desperately clung to the idea of staying married. It seemed he was putting my mother through mental torture, but she seemed determined not to give up until she was free of him.

Mom and I walked into the kitchen, and Lee set down her coffee cup, jumped out of her chair, and threw her arms around me. My heart soared to be back with them both. That semester marked the longest I'd been away from Lee since she'd come into our lives almost fifteen years earlier, and while I'd been away, I'd worried about her, stuck here in my parents' war.

"I have something to show you," I said. I reached into my purse and handed Lee the envelope.

"What have we here?" Lee slowly opened the envelope, and tears began to well in her eyes. "I'll be darned! A perfect report card!" She pulled me in for a hug so tight I almost lost my breath.

"Oh, Sandy! I am incredibly proud of you," Mom said. "Your father will be downstairs shortly, so you can show him your results." Her voice was light and happy, but I saw the worry in her eyes when she glanced at Lee.

Shortly afterward, Dad walked into the kitchen and over to the kitchen table. He sat down and picked up the newspaper, as if he wasn't aware of anyone else in the house.

I said, "Hi, Dad, it's good to see you."

As I leaned over to kiss his cheek, he turned his head away, so I made a kissing sound into the air and backed away, trying not to look hurt.

I looked around the kitchen and thought about how much older the house looked, kind of stiff and lifeless. I waited for

Dad to put the newspaper down, then I gently placed my report card in front of him. He stared at it in silence.

I'd done it. I'd risen to his challenge, and he was about to look inside that envelope and see the proof. All he needed to do was acknowledge my accomplishment and agree to stick to his part of the deal. My future hinged on one piece of paper, and my hands began to sweat.

He slipped the paper from the envelope and slowly scanned it from top to bottom. Then, without looking up, he tore up my all-A's report card and swept all the pieces of paper over the edge of the table into his palm, then turned around in his chair and threw it all in the trash.

"Letter grades mean nothing," he grumbled. "Show your worth through work. Get a job. College is a waste of money."

Across the kitchen, Lee looked horrified, her mouth agape. On the other side of the table, my mother looked like a statue, her hair stiff, her posture rigid, her eyes unblinking. I looked at her, silently begging her to say something, to do something. Pale and trembling, she spoke up. "Bob, you agreed to support her education if she received straight A's."

He looked at her and slammed his fist on the table. "I don't want to talk about it anymore. She's not going back to school." Then he pushed his chair back, its screeching sound echoing in my ears as he stormed out of the room.

I ran upstairs to my room and cried into my pillow. After I'd calmed down, I sat up and thought about my goals and my options. I wanted to go back to school and earn a college degree, that much was completely clear to me. Unclear was how I was going to accomplish that without the help of the father who never seemed to believe in me. That day I decided it didn't matter whether he believed in me because I believed in me. I declared to myself I'd go back to school and show him what a mistake he'd made by not investing in me. How I was going to do it without a penny of support from my parents was a knot I'd untangle another day.

It didn't take me long to realize I'd been caught in the middle of my parents' divorce and that my education had become one of my father's weapons against my mother. She wanted to raise independent, educated women. She wanted to make sure we never ended up like her, and he was going to punish her for it.

That night as I lay in bed, I heard my drunken father stumble home and into the master bedroom looking for a fight. By then, Mom had moved into Debbie's room on the other end of the house, but when she heard him making a racket, she stormed into the master bedroom and confronted him. Rob and I hid in the closet in my room as our parents screamed at each other about affairs and mistresses and college educations and broken promises. Eventually, they went quiet, and my brother said, "Sounds like he passed out."

I felt bad for Dad. He was making both himself and my mother miserable by not moving out, and as the months passed, he drank more and more. Even though he was a terrible husband, he was desperate to stay in our house and stay married. His stubbornness on this point was so strange to me—he was almost always "away on business," he was unfaithful to my mother, and when he was home, he spent most of his time snarling at his wife and kids, yet he fought like a badger to keep his life exactly as it was.

At the end of August, I returned to Arizona State and marched into the financial aid office, armed with loan applications all filled in and ready to file. I was going to do whatever it took to continue my studies. My number was called, and I approached the financial aid clerk, a middle-aged woman who sat slightly slumped.

With a big smile, I slid my papers across her desk. "I'd like to submit my financial aid application for fall tuition."

The clerk glanced at the application, then looked up at me. "I'm sorry, Ms. Krilich, but you missed the deadline for financial aid. You'll need to withdraw from your classes immediately to make room for other students."

"But I just got back from Chicago. I'm all ready to start my sophomore year."

"As I explained, if you're depending on financial aid, you missed the deadline. I'm afraid you won't be attending school this fall without your tuition paid in full."

It was a gut punch. Just like that, I'd been made a dropout, a failure. Overwhelmed by despair, I ran to the nearest bathroom in the building, hung my head over the toilet, and vomited, really vomited—the old-fashioned way, without any help from my finger. Now what was I going to do?

The next day there was a moving-out notice posted on my dorm door that read: *Dorms are for enrolled students only.* I'd been assigned a room when I registered for fall classes, but immediately after the financial aid clerk withdrew my registration for nonpayment of tuition, the housing office was notified, and they gave me two days to move out of the dorm.

I searched the Memorial Union housing wall where postings were listed for students searching for off-campus roommates and found an available room in a run-down, three-bedroom townhouse for sixty dollars a month. Two other Midwestern girls lived there, and they seemed nice enough, so I moved what little I had from the dorm to my new home, where the bathroom sink and toilet were permanently stained rust red, the aging refrigerator hummed like a diesel engine, and the cracked terra-cotta tile floors were covered in mildew. I'd used the last of my savings from working at Household Finance Corporation to pay the deposit and first month's rent, so I was now officially broke and without direction. But before going to bed that night, I stared in the mirror above my bathroom sink and saw the face of a powerful woman—tenacious and determined. I saw a woman who was going to figure out how to earn a college degree.

Strange as it seemed given my destitute circumstances, I felt happy to be on my own in the world. Mom sent me some money until I started earning my own, but I wanted to find a job fast. Some nights, my stomach growled and hurt because I could barely afford food, so for months I lived on popcorn and peanuts. It was my first experience with real hunger. I'd never realized that extreme hunger could lead to so many awful effects, like lightheadedness, fatigue, headaches, nausea, and even sadness.

I kept my focus on landing a job, but I didn't want just any job; I wanted to be a bank teller. I was determined to get some business experience.

After two weeks of filling out applications, I landed a full-time job as a teller at First Interstate Bank in Scottsdale and a second job at Federal Savings and Loan Bank in Tempe, working on Saturdays. Soon, I was busy and feeling optimistic, but I still had one big problem: my only means of transportation was a bicycle. It was a long ride to Scottsdale, and there were no bike lanes along the way. I wasn't afraid of riding a bike again; in fact, I couldn't wait to ride again after my accident. I didn't remember anything about being hit, only how much I loved the freedom of riding a bike, but I no longer trusted drivers. So I picked up a copy of *Auto Trader* at a local 7-Eleven and looked for a used motorcycle. I'd grown up riding dirt bikes around the property, so a motorcycle made the most sense to me. I found a Yamaha 250 for $500 and crossed my fingers I could save enough money to buy it before somebody else did.

Then I experienced a glorious moment of serendipity.

A few days after landing both jobs, I idled away in a Tempe strip mall, waiting for a friend to get a haircut. I wandered into a trophy shop, where a man approached the counter and in a strong Chicago accent said, "May I help you?"

"No thanks, just killing time," I said as I examined a volleyball.

"I detect a Midwest accent. Where are you from?"

"Wow, good ear. Barrington, Illinois, a small town north of—"

"I know Barrington. My old boss lives there."

"Who's your old boss?"

"Name was Robert Krilich. I worked for that son of a bitch for twenty-five years. He fired me for no reason."

I could feel my face flush hot. I wasn't used to hearing what people outside my family thought of my father, although I had a pretty good idea. I considered not telling this guy I was the daughter of that son of a bitch. Then I thought, what the hell?

"I'm so sorry. This is embarrassing, but that man you're talking about is my father."

"Your father! Wow, what a coincidence." He came out from behind the counter.

I asked, "Why did he fire you?" even though I'd already guessed why. My father was a builder/developer who sometimes accused people of theft, whether they'd stolen or not. I knew about this because he fired his brother-in-law for that reason, and it was humiliating for the entire family. I told the man this story, and he said, "Do you mean Al? Yeah, I knew about that debacle. What a son of a bitch, your father."

"You knew my uncle Al?"

"I did. Good guy. I'm Frank Retzke. Your father accused me of stealing some of his tools too. But I've never taken anything that wasn't mine. What's your name?"

"Sandy Krilich, his fifth daughter. My parents are divorcing after twenty-nine years. I've had to drop out of college for now until I can support myself. Dad won't help me pay for college anymore."

Frank took a step back, shaking his head and pressing his hand against his chest, his stubby fingers splayed out as he absorbed the revelation. "Your family and I go way back," he said. "I attended your christening and your brother's too."

"That's incredible!" I said.

"Well, I can't say I'm sorry to hear that your mother's free of him. Lillian is quite a lady."

"Yes, she is. She's going through a lot right now trying to get out of the marriage. Dad's fighting back hard, and one of his weapons was to stop paying for my education. He knew it would upset my mom like crazy."

"What a son of a bitch!" Frank said. "Sandy, I'd be happy to help you get through this challenging time. What can I do?"

I could feel tears starting to burn their way into my eyes. I didn't know a lot of really good men. I took a deep breath and said, "I hope to qualify for in-state tuition and secure a loan to finish school. And I just landed two jobs—at two different banks—but I only have a bicycle, and that's not going to do it. I came across a used Yamaha 250 for five hundred dollars. I know it's a lot to ask, but would you consider lending me five hundred dollars to buy the motorcycle? I can pay you back a hundred dollars a month."

"A motorcycle?" Frank said. "That sounds mighty dangerous. Do you know how to ride?"

"I've been riding dirt bikes since I was ten. I'm a good rider—probably better on a motorcycle than on a bicycle. I can promise I will be *very* careful."

"I remember when you were hit by a car," he said, shaking his head. "We all thought your father was going to have a heart attack that day."

Through the years, many people had told me about what a rough time my father had gone through after my devastating accident, but it was strange to hear their perspectives. The only time I remember feeling he was concerned for me was when he flew to the hospital in his new helicopter, another extravagance he had no need for. Although he was licensed to fly it, he usually let Charlie, his pilot friend, fly it for him, which I assumed was so he could drink as much as he wanted. Dad rarely came home sober.

One day as I lay in my hospital bed, I heard the *whup whup whup* of an incoming helicopter and looked out the window to see a helicopter landing on the hospital's parking garage. Dad hopped out of the enormous aircraft and dashed into the hospital like a surgeon late to somebody's life-or-death operation. A nurse also watching out the window said, "Your father must really love you." In that moment, I felt important to my dad. I felt special. The feeling didn't last long.

Frank said, "I'd be honored to give you a loan, and you can pay me back a hundred dollars at a time, when you can."

I reached for Frank's hand and began to cry. "I don't know how I'll ever be able to properly thank you for this."

Gripping my hand in a firm handshake, he said, "It's my pleasure. I understand your situation more than most would."

By the time my friend's haircut was finished, I'd signed a handwritten promissory note on the back of a blank sales receipt. I gave Frank a big hug, and when I walked out of that store, he felt like a dear uncle to me. Our encounter in a random strip mall in Tempe, Arizona, felt like an act of God.

Within six months, I'd paid Frank back in full.

In the spring of 1981, I was approved for financial aid after being declared independent because my father no longer used me as a tax deduction. And each semester after that I was given a $2,500 Pell Grant, which thrilled me because that was money I wouldn't have to pay back. I continued to work at First Interstate Bank for the rest of my college career and attended classes after work hours. Then, in May of 1985, I graduated with a bachelor's degree in finance, the same year my parents' divorce was finalized.

At the age of twenty-three, not long after I graduated from college, I dedicated myself to breaking free of the chains of bulimia and committed myself to a program for eating disorder recovery at La Mirada Hospital in Southern California. Every day I did the work, participating in intense group and individual therapy sessions, reflecting, and journaling to take a painfully honest look at myself to understand the core triggers of the disease. Dad and Mom visited, separately, on several occasions, and I appreciated their support. Then three months later, I walked out of La Mirada feeling healed and strong. During those three months, I'd managed to rewire my thinking, and from then on, I no longer engaged in self-destructive thinking. I was bursting with gratitude to have overcome a potentially deadly disorder at such a young age.

Just before my parents' divorce went through, Mom called to tell me the family home had been sold. The news was anticlimactic because it had taken so long to end the era of Rainbow Road. My siblings and I were so burned out by my parents' divorce drama and the painful memories we carried from some of the ugliness we'd experienced there that none of us went to the house to claim any belongings we'd left behind. Our mother was thrilled to be leaving that part of her life behind, but I had one big concern.

"Mom, what are Lee's plans after the house gets sold? Where will she go?"

"Oh, Sandy, Lee is coming with me! We're going to live together in my new home in Lake Barrington Shores."

An enormous wave of relief rushed through my body. "That's wonderful! I'm excited for you both. Can't wait to visit!"

Mom had grown up in a family of ten kids and hadn't lived alone at any point in her life. She and Lee were extremely compatible and comfortable around each other, so knowing they'd be together now without my toxic father poisoning the air gave me joy.

In November 1988, Mom attended the Republican National Convention in New Orleans, and it was there she met Bill Fraser. For the next sixteen years, she and Bill met for dinner twice a week, and now and then they'd take off together on a fishing trip. Lee loved Bill's humor, and the three of them often sat around Mom's kitchen table in the evenings, drinking cocktails and playing games, talking about the family, and watching the news, baseball, or movies. It was a happy home.

Part Three

Winter

"You think winter will never end, and then, when you don't expect it, when you have almost forgotten it, warmth comes and a different light."

WENDELL BERRY

$\underset{\displaystyle \sim\!\!\!\!\sim\!\!\!\!\sim}{}$ **13**

I n 1990, I was living in Los Angeles and working as the con-
troller for Tom, a generous real-estate billionaire. One Friday morning, he raced into my office.

"Sandy, I have a huge favor to ask. Something just came up
that I have to deal with. Can you take my place at the Hall of
Fame fundraiser at the Crowne Plaza Hotel? It's a lunch thing,
and there's going to be a guest speaker. I'd really appreciate it."

A free lunch? Why not? I said, "Absolutely, Tom. I'll leave
in a few minutes."

"One more thing—can you cut a check for a thousand dollars? It's a good cause."

"Sure, I'll have that ready for you to sign right away."

I passed Tom's office, he signed the check, and I left for the
event. I didn't know which Hall of Fame event I was supporting, but I was excited to get out of the office and happy to do
my boss a favor.

Fortunately, on that day I was especially well-dressed in a
new sky-blue suit, a white silk blouse, and dressy pumps, so I
knew I'd feel comfortable walking into an event where people
dropped one-thousand-dollar checks.

On my way to the hotel, I wondered if I'd recognize anyone at this fundraiser—Tom's events were usually a parade

of Who's Who. The last time I'd filled in for him had been at the opening of the Pantages Theatre in Hollywood. Back then, Tom owned the building, and he'd bought a table for ten, but all ten of his intended guests were relatives, and they all had to cancel at the last minute due to a family crisis. He'd asked if I'd attend on his behalf and fill the table with friends, which I did with little effort. It was a star-studded event: to the right were Steven Spielberg and Tom Cruise, and to the left Goldie Hawn and Kurt Russell. Everywhere I looked were faces I recognized from films I'd watched over the years.

Now I walked down a red carpet and into the luncheon room of the Crowne Plaza. I found Tom's name on the registration table where a young blonde woman wearing thick glasses and bright red lipstick handed me a name tag that had been prepared for me as Tom's replacement. On an easel outside the conference room was a huge sign that read: WELCOMING ERNIE BANKS TO LOS ANGELES.

I gasped and turned to the blonde woman. "*Ernie Banks* is the guest of honor?"

"Yes, he just flew in this morning. He'll be speaking at noon, so be sure you stay to hear him talk. He's a lovely man."

"Oh, I wouldn't miss it for anything!"

I *couldn't* believe it. *The* Ernie Banks was here. I was attending an event featuring Mr. Cub himself!

Ernie was known by many for breaking baseball's race barrier in 1953 by being the first Black man to play for the Chicago Cubs. But to me he was so much more. He was the player Lee loved most in the world. From what I could tell, he might have been the *person* she loved most in the world.

In the event room, I found my table, which was filled with Tom's business associates. I sat next to Peter, whom I knew because of various deals we'd both worked on, then I glanced around to see if I could spot Ernie Banks. And there he was, seated just three tables away, wearing a black suit, a white shirt, and a blue tie. His smile was as bright as I recalled from watching him on TV and studying his pictures in Lee's room.

I wanted to run to a phone to call Lee. I knew she'd be home in Barrington because she rarely left my mom's house. But I decided against it. I thought I should first come up with a plan to meet Ernie Banks, after which I'd be able to tell Lee all about it. I knew that would make her dizzy with joy. But what would I say to this man who had meant the world to Lee, this man whose signed pictures and books had lined the walls of her rooms for the past twenty-five years?

A quick-footed hotel staff served fresh romaine and mandarin salads, and in between bites, I made small talk with Peter, who'd been a big Mr. Cub fan during his childhood. Then came the chicken entrée, and as the minutes ticked by, I realized I was running out of time to figure out how to meet the legendary guest of honor. I thought, should I walk over there and interrupt him during his lunch? Would everyone think me rude? Would Ernie? Did he have bodyguards?

Too late. As dessert was being served, the emcee walked onstage and began to speak.

"Good afternoon, ladies and gentlemen. I'd like to share some facts about our guest of honor. In 1953, at the age of twenty-two, Ernie Banks of Dallas, Texas, was the first Black player to sign with the Chicago Cubs, and he stayed with the

Cubs organization for the next eighteen years—his entire major league career. In 1977, Ernie was inducted into the National Baseball Hall of Fame, and in 1999, he was named to the Major League Baseball All-Century Team. We're all here today to support Ernie's lifelong passion, the Live Above and Beyond Foundation, which helps struggling youth and the elderly with their health-care needs. Because of his efforts, a lot of people feel healthy and valued. Every penny donated here today will go to support Ernie's foundation. And now, it is with great pleasure that I introduce to you the one and only Ernie Banks."

Everyone in the room stood up and cheered, and already my heart swelled with love for this man I'd never met. We stood for what seemed like ten minutes while Ernie passed behind me, walked up a few stairs, and made his way to the podium.

I so wished Lee was by my side. I wanted desperately to turn this lucky day into something more than just an Ernie Banks sighting. I wanted to find a way to connect with him, so I could give her joy as I told her all about it. I vowed to find a way to talk to him.

Ernie spoke. "I am honored and deeply grateful to be here today, and I'd like to start my speech by saying that our success is not only dependent upon the talent God gives us but also upon the people who believe in us. This is certainly true as it pertains to my baseball career. Sure, I was the one who played the game, but I wouldn't be here today if it weren't for the people who believed in me and gave me the encouragement to play."

He stood up tall and straight and seemed completely comfortable talking to the captivated audience. He talked about the joy of playing for the Chicago Cubs and how grateful he was to all the fans who had made his career a success. The fans were what it was all about, he said.

When he finished speaking, everyone stood again and clapped and cheered. It was obvious he was beloved, even here in this hotel conference room in Los Angeles, well across the country from the Wrigley Field he called home.

He walked off the stage and returned to his seat at the luncheon table. *Oh, he's just right over there,* I thought. *I'm so close!* I took a long sip from my glass of wine, hoping to gather enough liquid courage to approach the sports legend I was sure everyone in the room wanted to talk to. But every time I glanced his way, he was wrapped up in conversation.

I kept checking my watch, getting more and more nervous I was going to miss my chance.

Then came my opening! The woman sitting in the chair next to Ernie's got up and walked toward the ballroom's exit. I took a deep breath, stood up, and hustled over to his table. Miraculously, he was alone when I arrived by his side, so I cleared my throat and dove in.

"Excuse me, pardon me, Ernie, Mr. Banks? May I speak to you for a moment?" I was sure he'd give me a quick, polite dismissal. Ugh, I should have had more wine.

"Absolutely," he said with a big smile, gesturing to the open chair next to him. "Sit on down. I'd love to talk."

Now I was genuinely in love. I sat down. "Mr. Banks—"

"Call me Ernie."

I smiled and could feel my face getting warmer. "Ernie, I'm Sandy, and I'm from Chicago too. I'd like to tell you about someone incredibly special to me, someone who might be the biggest fan you've ever had. Her name is Lee Metoyer. She helped raise me and still lives with our family. I guess you could say that Lee *is* our family. She's a huge Cubs fan and has adored you all her life."

"Well, isn't that somethin'? I am honored," Ernie said, his eyes locked on mine.

"I think Lee would have a heart attack if she knew I was talking to you right now!"

"Oh no, let's hope that doesn't happen," Ernie said, looking genuinely concerned. Then his face brightened again, and he said, "Tell me more about Lee."

I turned my chair to face him. "Lee has a big autographed picture of you in her bedroom. One Christmas, all she wanted was your *Mr. Cub* book. And she's recorded the stats for every Cubs game played since 1965. If you want any of your game statistics, she can rattle them off, *from memory.*"

He laughed. "Well, she sounds like someone I'd love to talk to. If you have her number, I'll give her a call."

For a second, I thought my heart had stopped. "Wow!" I gushed. "You'd really call her? Oh, Mr. Ba . . . Ernie . . . that would just make her day. It would make her year, her life! How can I possibly thank you?"

"*I* want to thank Lee for being so committed to the Chicago Cubs and for being such a great fan of mine. She sounds like an exceptional person." He placed a napkin in front of me. "Please write her name and number here, and I'll take care of it. Thank you so much for telling me about her. I'm looking forward to our talk."

I was shaking as I wrote the number for the house phone at Mom and Lee's home. Then I checked the number three times to make sure I'd written it correctly and clearly. "Thank you, Ernie," I said, handing him the napkin. "But wait, I need to warn you, she's not going to believe it's you. She may even accuse you of pulling a prank, so you might need to tell her something specific about yourself."

"Okay, I will, but don't let her know I'm going to call. Let's make it a surprise."

"As hard as it will be to keep this from her, I will! It's our secret," I said.

After I left the event, I knew I was going to be a bundle of nerves until I heard from Lee. How long was I going to have to wait? A day? A week? Longer? This was going to be unbearable. But it was the most joyful, painful anticipation I'd ever experienced. I prayed and prayed Ernie Banks would follow through on his promise.

Two days later, Lee called. "Sandy!" she shouted. "I talked to him! *Ernie Banks!* I can't believe it. When I realized it was him, I almost fell off my chair. At first, I thought it was a prank call, but when he told me he grew up in Dallas and had hit his five-hundredth home run on May 12, 1970, I knew it was him. I remember that day like it was yesterday. *The* Ernie Banks! *My* Ernie Banks!"

"Aw, Lee, that's wonderful," I said. "I met him at a fundraiser. It was kind of a fluke that I was there at all. Anyway, when I found out Ernie Banks was the guest of honor, I could hardly wait to tell you. I told him all about you, and I just about died when he asked for your phone number. How long did you two speak to each other?"

"For over thirty minutes!" Lee said. "It was the best thirty minutes of my life!"

"That's incredible!" Then I laughed. "Wait, what could you two possibly talk about for thirty minutes?"

"Are you kidding? We talked about baseball stats, then changes in the game because of betting and multimillion-dollar player contracts. It's become a business rather than a game. We both said how grateful we are to have been born at a time when we could experience the true essence of the game. Then he thanked me for all my support for the Chicago Cubs and for supporting his game," Lee gushed with breathless delight.

I said, "He's a wonderful man, and he has a foundation that helps young people and the elderly get things they need, like health-care coverage."

"I'm so glad to hear that. It's so good to know he's as wonderful as I always believed him to be."

Before we hung up, Lee's voice became quieter, and she sounded as if she was about to cry. "I just had a conversation with *Ernie Banks*. My life is complete."

My eyes filled with tears. I couldn't think of a better gift I could have given her, this selfless person who had been everything to my family and who asked for nothing. It was one of the greatest days of my life.

Three years later, in 1993, Lee was diagnosed with lung cancer, and Mom became Lee's caregiver. She made sure Lee ate well, accompanied her to doctor visits, and managed her medications. In the evenings, she and Lee watched movies together. My mother considered it a privilege to be there in this way for the woman who had been her closest friend and confidante during the best and worst times of her life.

As Lee's illness worsened, I visited and stayed for several days at a time, helping with whatever Mom and Lee needed. One day as I was cleaning Lee's bedroom, she said, "You know, Sandy, I owe your mother so much. I could never thank her for all she's done for me."

"I don't get it," I said. "You worked for us all those years, loyal to your last day, and devoted your life to helping our family. Shouldn't she be thanking you?"

"Honey, I know you don't understand, but your mother saved my life."

"What do you mean?"

"I can't explain it, but your mother is the best thing that ever happened to me."

"That's lovely. And please know that it goes both ways. You are by far the best thing that ever happened to our family."

"Thank you, sweetheart. That means a lot to me. Now I'm going to lie down. I'm getting tired."

"Sweet dreams." I closed her door and left her to sleep.

Lee died a year later.

In August 1989, one year before I met Ernie Banks, I went to a party in Long Beach, and shortly after entering the event, I spotted a tall, handsome guy across the room. His name was Karl, and we clicked immediately. We spent the rest of the evening talking, dancing, and ignoring everyone else at the party. Soon afterward we began a long-distance relationship, which involved a lot of time on the road as he lived in Santa Barbara and I was in LA. After two years of commuting up and down the California coast, we married in Chicago.

Karl was the kind of man I'd dreamed of: outgoing, intelligent, independent, and ambitious. And he radiated confidence, which I found especially attractive because I had so little of it myself. Immediately after our honeymoon, Karl's work called for us to move to Singapore and after that Australia. In 1995, Kyle and Lexi, our twins, were born in Melbourne, where we lived until they were four years old. Then we moved back to the States, and the kids and I stayed with Mom in Barrington while Karl tried to find us a home in The Woodlands, a suburb north of Houston.

One morning while Mom and I were having coffee, she started telling stories about the elaborate Fourth of July parties she and Dad threw every year. They hired a full band, and they roasted lambs on a rotisserie, Croatian style, for more than a hundred people who spread out all over the back patio and house.

"Your father really loved a party," she said. "He loved being wrapped up in the show, working the room, charming everybody."

I remember well how my father behaved at those parties. With his high-gelled hair and sideburns and that swagger, I thought he looked like something between Elvis and James Dean. When the band played fifties music, he jitterbugged like a madman.

I treasured these adult conversations with Mom, especially now that the drama and pain of our family life was behind us. "He sure was different with us, though," I told her. "So sunny and dynamic with party guests. Where was that fun guy when his kids were around?"

"Your father never understood how to have healthy relationships. And he tried to escape his demons through work and partying."

I considered what she meant by "demons." I knew he was unpredictable and often angry, and he rarely seemed fulfilled, never quietly content. I wondered what kind of demons tortured him. What went on in his past that had made him so bitter?

"We did have some good times in the Barrington house," my mother said. "Not all good, of course. Some very bad. Very bad."

I wondered what she was thinking about in that moment, but then my mind flashed back to the horrible day when our caretaker, Mrs. Batista, had been so terribly burned. I asked, "Did you ever find out why their car exploded by the gas pump? Why didn't we ever get any answers about that?"

She sighed. "It's been long enough. I suppose I can tell you what your father told me. But first let me give you some context. At the time of the explosion, the Feds were cracking down on corruption in Chicago. It was quite widespread, and one day your father was in the wrong place at the wrong time and witnessed a government bribe. He was asked to admit to what he'd seen, but he knew if he squealed on the people involved, his career would be over, especially because at the time he was an up-and-coming builder. So he kept quiet, which clearly ticked off the Feds."

"What does this have to do with the explosion?" I asked.

"The explosion was a warning to your father to talk, or else."

I shouldn't have been surprised. My father had a secret life and did time in prison, after all. But this was like listening to a description of a Mob movie. "Did he talk?" I asked.

"No, so they put him away for tax evasion. He said they'd hoped the threat of prison would make him talk, but he wouldn't."

"My God, that poor family went through hell. And because of Chicago corruption that had absolutely nothing to do with them? Mrs. Batista was in agony, and her kids were terrified."

"I know, dear. It was just horrible."

I didn't even know where to direct my anger about that shocking news. I shook my head and said, "They were innocent. I pray they all recovered completely."

What a rusty shack of secrets my father's life was. The more I heard about him, the more I realized I barely knew him at all. There was a period after Mom and Dad divorced when Dad tried to get close to me. He called almost every day to ask about my work and to share his ideas for new deals he was working on. What a switch—the guy who didn't think me worthy of a college education now wanted to tell me about business deals he had in the works. He planned ski trips that included all his kids, plus partners. We seemed like a regular family, skiing during the days and going to dinner or watching movies in the evenings. It seemed to me he tried to get close to all of us to ease the pain of his marriage ending.

Even though my father warmed up to me after his divorce, there was no undoing the damage he inflicted throughout my childhood. I knew no other fathers who were so hard on their kids. *Why*, why did he yell at us and bully us and just plain neglect us? I've tried to piece together what I know of his past to help me understand. He didn't speak of his childhood, but through the years I heard stories about alcohol abuse in his childhood home. And violence.

My father did tell me that when he was a teenager his best friend drowned while they were swimming together in Lake Michigan. An undertow dragged the boy out, and Dad couldn't save him. My father never fully recovered from the loss, which was followed by a lifetime of survivor's guilt.

Born in 1930, my father grew up in a household that had been battered by the Depression, and I know that's why he was driven to make so much money. His impoverished upbringing caused him to constantly cut back on expenses in our household, but outside the home, he wanted the world to see how much he had, so he showed off his wealth with multiple houses, boats, cars, a helicopter, and a plane.

As I assume is the case with most adults, I came to view my father a bit more gently after I was out of the family house and living on my own. My father's parenting was informed by the parenting he received, so he had very few positive tools to bring to the project. Some people vow to break a cycle of abuse and neglect, while others perpetrate it. Very unfortunately for my mother, my siblings, and me, my father didn't break the hostile cycle he'd been part of as a boy. But I know his life was a complicated one. He must have felt empty at his center to need so many possessions, so many showy things, and to live so many lies.

While Mom was dating Bill, I experienced the protective care of a fatherly figure for the first time. Bill always wanted me to be at the airport two hours before my flight, and he'd call me to confirm I'd left for the airport. He discouraged me from staying out late. And when I was engaged to Karl, he told me not to spend time with my male friends without Karl around. He said, "An engaged woman doesn't mingle with other men." His values were strict and very old-fashioned, but I knew his intentions were good, and he made me feel watched over and cared for.

After sixteen years of dating, Mom and Bill married in 2004. They were both seventy-nine, and she was a stunning bride in a shimmering gold dress. I told her she would have been perfect as a cover model for a story about how it's never too late to get married. My ten-year-old twins were there to witness the joyous occasion, and I was grateful they had never watched their grandmother go through her awful years with their grandfather. The newlyweds moved from Lake Barrington Shores to a cozy one-story home less than a mile away.

Bill passed away unexpectedly four months after their wedding. Mom was devastated by the loss, and she spent the next four years living alone for the first time in her life. She looked forward to our calls and visits, and she traveled often, visiting her kids in Texas, Utah, and Arizona. Roseann lived close to Mom, but she was very busy raising four girls, so Mom made a lot of effort to form deep relationships with her grandchildren, which was a priceless gift to all of us.

In December 2008, four years after Bill's death, Mom was diagnosed with pancreatic cancer. She died ten weeks later, and my siblings and I were completely unprepared for the sudden loss of the person who still held us all together. Mom's death pushed me into a mid-life crisis, and I realized I no longer wanted to work in corporate finance, but I wasn't sure what to do next. I just knew I needed a change. I prayed and did a lot of soul-searching, asking God to guide my next steps.

A year after Mom's death, my siblings and I sold her house, and I spent a lot of time sorting out her affairs. Then, the day before we were to turn over possession of the house to the new owners, something launched my life in an entirely new direction.

$\approx\!\!\approx\!\!\approx$ 14

A fter we sold our mother's house, it was time to close the door to the place Mom and Bill had called home, so all six of us kids gathered to clean it out. Roseann and Robin still lived in the Chicago area, and I flew in from Houston, Debbie from Utah, Barb from Scottsdale, and Rob from Las Vegas. We'd already sold the valuable furniture, so what remained were Mom's and Lee's belongings, heirlooms, and various household items. We started in the early morning and vowed to finish in one day, no matter how many hours it took. Debbie was in charge, and that morning she assigned each of us a room and told us to decide whether each item left in the room was something we should keep or dispose of. It was an emotional task, sifting through the possessions our mother had treasured for years.

We separated the items into three categories: keepsakes for the family, items to donate, and trash. As we worked, we unearthed a trove of memories—a worn baking pan that brought back the memory of Mom's pineapple upside-down cake, a box of her cherished recipes, delicate strands of rosaries.

While sifting through Mom's beautiful wardrobe, Debbie had an idea. "Why don't we pick one of her favorite outfits and cut it into six pieces to carry with us as a keepsake?"

"How will we choose the outfit?" I asked.

"Each of us can pick two dresses and then we can vote."

After sifting through her clothes, it was clear which dress we all wanted to share. It was a dress Mom had worn for years to birthday celebrations, graduations, and weddings. The dress was flowy with swirls of pinks, aqua blues, leaf greens, and mustard yellows, all fantastically bright and cheerful, like her.

Debbie pulled a pair of scissors from the kitchen drawer and started cutting the dress into six pieces. Then she handed each of us our piece, saying, "Cherish this piece as a memory of our beautiful mother's bright spirit."

After I finished cleaning out Mom's office, I moved to the basement, where I found Lee's belongings. In the dimly lit space, I rummaged through the baseball scorebooks in which she chronicled every game she'd watched from 1965 to 1994. There must have been thousands of them. I found the three autographed photographs of Ernie Banks she'd hung on her bedroom wall, now in padded envelopes for preservation. Also in the trunk were her Sidney Sheldon books, baseball collectibles, and six dozen romance novels. Inside a smaller chest were Lee's Bible, crossword books, dictionaries, photo albums full of pictures from each of our weddings, the two photographs of her husband and boy, and the patent leather radio she carried faithfully to every baseball game. It awed me that she'd lived so simply, that she had so few possessions. Everything Lee had treasured was here or represented right here in front of me.

The six of us spent the entire day taking the last of the belongings from the house. The sun sank low as we gathered in the driveway next to the fully packed moving truck that would be headed for Goodwill first thing in the morning and then to a small storage unit to store the sentimental items. Everyone was tired and hungry, so Barb and I said we'd be quick as we did a final walk-through to check every last inch.

Sure enough, we'd missed something. Standing in front of Mom's closet, I pointed up toward a white box, tucked in the far corner of the upper shelf. It was the only thing left in the house.

"Maybe it's one of Mom's empty hat boxes," I said.

"Sure looks like it," Barb said. She pulled down the box and handed it to me. Whatever was inside was heavier than a hat. I settled on the carpet, placed the box on my lap, and peeled back the lid. Inside was a round silver tin decorated with a formal, inscribed label. When I read the label, I felt a bolt of adrenaline surge through my abdomen and chest. *Lee Metoyer, Cremation date: October 24, 1994.*

Barb and I both held our breath as if holding it would somehow suspend the weight of what we'd just uncovered. I had no idea Mom had kept Lee's ashes in safekeeping in her closet all this time. After Lee's service fifteen years earlier, we'd held a celebration of life dinner, and at that point Mom hadn't yet received Lee's remains from the funeral home, so there had been no discussion about where the ashes should be kept or scattered. After the service, we all went back to our lives and forgot about the subject of Lee's remains.

As I sat there absorbing the significance of what I held in my hands, I remembered my promise to Lee.

Oh, dear God, the promise!

I'd promised to write her story. But we hadn't had time for her to tell me anything about *the story*. We hadn't had even one short conversation about this mysterious past she wanted me to convert to prose and share with the world. As vehement as

Lee had been about not wanting to be asked about her past, in the end, she'd seemed equally vehement that I share her story, that I even develop it into a book. Now I wondered what the reversal had been about. And what had gone on in her earlier years that had been so painful or dark or shameful that she clamped down whenever she was asked even the most superficial questions about her life? Why the change of heart as she saw the end was near? And *what* on earth was I supposed to do now? Where was I going to start?

I tried to take it in, there as I sat in my deceased mother's home, physically cradling the remains of Lee, our Lee, my Lee, my second mother and the greatest source of strength and stability in my life and my mother's life. She was here in this little silver tin. I held the cold tin in my hands and decided I'd just have to start somewhere. The first step was to round up my siblings and come up with a plan.

Barb called the others back inside from the U-Haul, and we gathered in the foyer. My exhausted siblings shot me puzzled looks as I stood there cradling the white box, my eyes filled with tears. As the moon cast an ethereal glow through the windows, Barb pointed to the box and explained, "We just found this up in Mom's closet. It's Lee's ashes. We need to decide what to do with them."

They were all quiet for a moment, then Roseann spoke softly. "We should do the right thing, the honorable thing."

Robin asked, "What's the right thing? Do you mean we should split her ashes six ways?"

Barb, ever faithful, said, "Let us trust in God to guide us."

I waited until they'd all spoken, then cleared my throat and said, "Remember, Lee always said if the Cubs ever won the World Series, she wanted some of her ashes sprinkled on Wrigley Field."

Rob laughed. "Ha! Like that's ever going to happen!"

Debbie said, "Why don't we find where her husband and son are buried and lay her to rest with them?"

Of course! All those years she'd pined for them, only two little photos on a dresser to keep her connected with her beloved husband and her precious little boy, both taken from her so prematurely. The idea of reuniting Lee with her loved ones felt so very right to me. But I also wanted to honor her request about Wrigley Field. Maybe we could save a small bit of her ashes in case the Cubs ever won the World Series. It was a long shot, but I thought we owed it to Lee.

It felt as if a sacred mission was unfolding before us, a pilgrimage of sorts. But who would undertake it? Which of us had the time to dig into Lee's background to find where her husband and son were buried?

I knew the answer, of course. I was the one who'd made the colossal promise to Lee fifteen years earlier. I was the obvious choice.

Robin said, "Sandy could do it. She was really close to Lee."

Debbie asked, "Sandy, do you have time for a research project like this?"

I'd just left my job at Anadarko as a financial analyst and had been scrambling to reclaim my lost sense of purpose. I couldn't imagine a more meaningful endeavor than this one. In the process, maybe I'd learn why she'd been so tight-lipped about her family all those years. Maybe by learning the story of the boy and his father, I'd find out what was at the heart of her ferocious secrecy.

"I'll do it," I said, trying to sound confident.

Debbie declared it official. "Sandy will research to find out where Lee's husband and son are buried . . ."

"And they'll be together again," Barb added. Her words hung over the six of us like a hopeful prayer.

⚞⟐ **15**

I said goodbye to my mother's house and flew home to Houston with Lee's ashes in my suitcase. It was a bittersweet moment when halfway into the flight, I realized this was Lee's first time on a plane, the first time she'd ever soared through the sky, above the clouds. She would have loved being on a plane, and I could picture her being served by a flight attendant, then offering to clean up, telling the staff not to fuss over her and saying she was just happy to be there. I would have loved to have watched her amazement as she marveled at the sight of the land from the sky.

The instant the wheels touched the ground in Texas, it felt as if the clock had started ticking. Lee's ashes needed to go home where they belonged.

That night, I told Karl and the kids about my new mission. Lexi and Kyle had questions.

"Why search for dead people that have been gone for decades?" Lexi asked.

"I think it would be an honor to reunite Lee with her loved ones and to lay her to rest," I said.

"But they won't know they're reunited. They're dead," Kyle said.

Karl smiled from across the table. He often left me to sift through the more philosophical questions.

"It's not about whether they know or not," I said. "It's about honoring Lee. And I think everyone should be near their loved ones when they're laid to rest."

"But if it's just ashes, how are you going to bury her with them? You can't dig up the caskets, can you?" Lexi asked.

I looked at Karl. He just kept smiling and focusing on his dinner. "Oh no, honey," I said. "My siblings and I will have a little ceremony for Lee, say some prayers, and then sprinkle her ashes on top of the graves. The Bible says 'to dust we will return,' so she'll share the same soil as her loved ones."

"That's weird, Mom," Kyle said.

"Think of it this way, when I die, I want to be near Dad and you two because we're family. Lee's husband and son are her family."

"That makes sense," Lexi said.

Karl smiled at me, and I knew we were both thinking about what a sweet pleasure it is when a teenager is agreeable.

That night, after everyone was asleep, I typed *Metoyer family* into a Google search, and I was surprised when a detailed timeline popped up, unveiling the Metoyer Era—a historic period long before Lee's time. I felt my pulse start to race.

I read that the Metoyers were people of French and African descent and that from 1796 to 1847 they migrated to Natchitoches, Louisiana, where the Creole culture was founded. They had once lived on the illustrious Melrose Plantation, a mansion nestled alongside the serene Cane River. Wow, I thought, Lee was Creole, and her people had lived in a mansion! The article revealed that during the seventeenth and eighteenth centuries, the Metoyers were one of the wealthiest Creole families around, and the Melrose Plantation was later transformed into a museum that still preserves the rich heritage of the Metoyer family.

Right away, the search felt like a fascinating research project, and how thrilling it was to learn about someone I actually knew. Had I just now discovered Lee's roots? Or was this line of Metoyers completely unrelated to her? Until now, I'd known nothing about Lee's name, and the only thing I knew about her background was what she told me one afternoon when I'd been curious because in history class, we'd been talking about nationalities.

Lee and I were cleaning the glasses behind the bar, and I asked, "What's your family's ancestry?" Over the years, I'd tried to adhere to the *don't ask Lee about her past* rule, but sometimes I ventured a question. This one seemed harmless.

"We're half French and half African American," she said. Then, uncharacteristically, she said more. "A long time ago, my family was important."

"What do you mean 'important'?"

"We had a . . . territory." She hesitated. "But we lost it, and that's why my family moved to Chicago."

A *territory*! As far as I knew, territories were the holdings of the elite, of aristocrats, of kings and queens. "A territory!" I gushed. "I guess your family was *important*."

"That was a long time ago, way before my time," Lee said. "Let's finish these glasses so I can help your mother with dinner."

As I lay in bed that night, I turned to Karl. "I think we need to take a drive."

"Where?" he asked, half asleep.

"I just found something interesting about Lee's ancestors. Turns out a family of Metoyers are from a famous plantation in Louisiana called the Melrose Plantation, and now it's a museum!"

"How far is this place?" Karl asked.

"It's about a four-hour drive east, but we're already going that way for the concert. What if we just keep going and visit the place?"

"That may work. We can talk about it in the morning," he said, then rolled over and fell asleep.

I knew Karl would be up for the road trip. The idea of chasing history had always sparked his interest. Many evenings after a long day of work, he planted himself in front of the television to travel back in time by watching the History Channel.

The next morning, Karl and I sat in the kitchen drinking coffee, and to my delight, after a night of sleep, Karl had a lot more enthusiasm for the adventure. "This is right up my alley," he said. "And maybe we can take Lee's ashes just in case we stumble upon their graves in Louisiana."

"Great idea."

I thought about how extraordinary it would be to reach that goal so quickly. But the idea of it also left me feeling a bit hollow. Lee had already told me about her family having owned territory. Where was the big mysterious story in that? It was centuries ago, Lee had said. Already, I questioned whether I'd be able to honor Lee's deathbed request.

As Karl and I drove along the quiet country roads of Texas and Louisiana, I looked out the window and thought back to when Lee and I had watched the TV series *Roots*. Karl and I were now in the Deep South, a place I knew about only because of that show. Every year, Lee insisted we watch *Roots*, but when I watched it for the first time at age fifteen, it hit me so hard, months passed before I could go a day without thinking about it.

In January 1977, *Roots* aired for the first time. Chicago had been in the middle of an extraordinarily long string of sub-freezing days and nights, and to get ready to settle in for the evening, I'd bundled in my coat and boots, headed outside to gather logs, then lit a fire in the family room fireplace. Snuggled under a cozy flannel blanket, Lee gripped a mug of steaming Irish coffee and laid down some ground rules.

"Okay, first of all, no interruptions during the show. Don't ask any questions until the commercial breaks, and please refrain from picking up the phone," she said, her forehead pinched in seriousness.

I raised my eyebrows. "What's this show about, anyway?"

"It's about an African American family. It's the story of a family that originally came from Africa and then lived in the South. No talking for any reason during the show. Only emergencies, but otherwise, no talking."

I wanted to watch *Roots* because I knew how important it was to Lee and because she wanted company. But I hadn't read anything about the series, so I was expecting a sweet story of a family that moved to America for a new life, maybe a heart-warming rag-to-riches tale. Oh, how wrong I'd been.

The story's protagonist, Kunta Kinte, portrayed by LeVar Burton, was a Mandinka youth who had been kidnapped in West Africa and sold into slavery. I flinched and my eyes watered as Kunta was whipped and when the kidnappers demanded he say his new slave name, Toby, which his owner's wife had assigned. The longer I watched, the more my stomach churned. At the same time, I marveled that Kunta, a young man so close to my age, could be so strong in spirit, that his loyalty to his family name and roots were unbreakable.

As Lee and I watched the series together for eight days, I looked over at her many times. She was always focused on the show, her face still, her hands in her lap. I don't remember our talking about the show in between episodes or even after it was over, but I remember being uncomfortable not understanding why it moved Lee so deeply. Had anyone in her family been enslaved?

Why wasn't I ever allowed to ask about Lee's history?

At the entrance to the Melrose Plantation, Karl drove us down a paved road to a gravel road and across a small bridge that crossed the Cane River. Then there it was, the magnificent plantation upon a sprawling estate of trees. On the wraparound porch sat two wooden rocking chairs set to look out over the sprawling foliage. I knew this majestic Creole was now a tourist site, but the home looked as if it was still lived in.

I scanned the property and took in the open fields dotted with little cottages, decaying buildings, and a large graveyard behind a magnificent ancient Catholic church. We drove over a bridge and passed another field before we turned into the parking lot of the plantation. After paying the parking fee, we found the gift shop, where a lady with short, dark hair and very white teeth greeted us. The tag pinned to her shirt read: *Juliette Metoyer*. Could *she* be one of Lee's relatives?

I said, "Hello. Do you happen to have any information on the Metoyer family?"

Juliette's eyes sparkled. "Oh my, we have a *wealth* of information here in our book section. May I ask what has sparked your interest in the Metoyers?"

"I'm here to research the history of Lee Metoyer. She was a second mother to me. Lee was a very private person and never spoke of her relatives, so I'm hoping to find out if she's connected to the Metoyers from this plantation."

"Well, isn't this exciting! Most people who pass through here have no connection to the Metoyers. I have the perfect book for you to begin your research." Juliette handed me *The Forgotten People of Cane River*, by Gary B. Mills.

I took one look at the cover and gasped. The resemblance between the woman in the picture on the book's cover and Lee was astonishing. Both had dark brown hair, latte-colored skin, friendly hazel eyes, and a sweet smile. The woman even seemed to be wearing a maid's uniform.

"The woman on this book cover, who is she?" I asked.

Juliette smiled. "That's Marie Thérèse, also known as Coincoin. She was the matriarch of the Metoyer family, the mother of all mothers. Her story is captivating. You'll find it all there in the book—an extraordinary lineage, indeed." She went on to explain that the sprawling land around us was the legacy of Pierre Metoyer and his concubine, Marie Thérèse Metoyer.

"Do you know if there's any documentation of a family tree associated with Coincoin?" I asked.

Juliette nodded and handed me another book. "This is *Isle of Canes*, written by Elizabeth Shown Mills, Gary's wife. It's the fictionalized account Elizabeth wrote of the Creole people after Gary died. You'll find a family tree in there that shows the beginning of the Metoyer line in the 1700s."

I started to flip through the book until I found the family tree. I turned to Juliette. "These family trees don't show the more recent generations. Do you have anything that shows the Metoyer lineage from Coincoin up to today?"

She handed me a thick blue-and-white book called *The Metoyers*.

"Here we have a book that documents every current descendant of Coincoin and Pierre Metoyer, a comprehensive record of the Metoyer family. It's a pricey one, one hundred dollars."

I gasped as I took the book from her. "Wow, this is heavy! If you don't mind, I'd like to sit for a few minutes to see if I can find Lee's name in here. If I'm lucky, maybe it will have her family listed as well."

"I don't mind at all. Let me know if you need my help."

Karl bought tickets for the tour while I settled into a seat in the bookstore. My hand shook as I turned the pages. This was extraordinary—one Google search got me here, and already I was holding a book that might reveal some of the secrets of Lee's past. Maybe in this book, I'd learn something about whatever it was she thought should be developed into a book of her own.

I flipped to the index in the back and saw a lot of Metoyers listed, then ran my finger down the list looking for Lee's name. And there it was!

I moved backward from Lee's name to the starting point of the branch of the tree Lee descended from. The first person listed was Pierre, but it wasn't Pierre, the patriarch; it was his son, Pierre Metoyer II (1772–1833), the fourth child of Coincoin and Pierre. From there, the line continued to his son, Pierre Metoyer III (1806–1906), followed by Joseph Pamphile Metoyer (1843–1887). Joseph Pamphile Metoyer was the father of Ernest Avnar Pamphile Metoyer (1869–1941), who was Lee's grandfather. Ernest's son, Joseph Arnold Metoyer (1892–1944) was Lee's father. Joseph married Evelyn (Sudie Mae) Simon (1893–1942). After Joseph and Evelyn, Lee and all her siblings were listed. My heart leapt when I saw the name Hazel. Lee had told me she'd had a sister named Hazel who had taught her how to clean.

I couldn't believe it! There it all was in black and white—Lee's family, her history, her people!

Then I realized something was missing. After the names of Lee's siblings, their spouses and children were listed. I turned to Juliette. "Is there a reason there's no mention of a spouse or child next to Lee's name? She was married and had a son, both of whom died tragically in a car accident."

She pursed her lips. "Well, that's confusing. This is meant to be a comprehensive account of the Metoyer family. Do you know if Lee and her husband were legally married? And did their son have an official birth certificate?"

My heart sank as I admitted, "I don't have that information. How would I even go about finding out?"

"You might want to start with Vital Records. They maintain all source documents, such as birth and death certificates, marriage licenses, separation agreements, and divorce certificates. Most of the Metoyer book came from those records—plus some earlier sources for the historical content."

"Thank you. I really appreciate your help," I said, then got lost in the book again, jotting notes as I read.

Lee was only twenty years old when she lost her mother in 1942, and her father passed away two years later. How awful, I thought. So young to lose both parents. I wondered how they had died so young and just two years apart. And what did Lee do then? Where did she live after her parents died? Had she been telling the truth all along, that her entire family was all gone? But what about her siblings, nieces, and nephews? Certainly, some of them must be alive, I thought.

Juliette's voice interrupted my rumbling train of silent questions. "Your tour is going to begin in three minutes. You can join your group down the cobblestone pathway, near the fountain."

I handed the enormous book back to her and bought both of the Mills' books. I couldn't wait to dig in and find out more about Coincoin, Pierre, and the rest of the Metoyer family. I was starting to think like a detective.

The tour consisted of ten visitors and Sam, a clean-cut thirtysomething tour guide, who encouraged us to ask questions. After introducing himself, he said, "We'll be exploring the historically rich land once occupied by the Metoyer family."

Just the mention of the Metoyer name thrilled me. I squeezed Karl's hand as Sam continued. "The years 1796 to

1847 mark the Metoyer Era here at the Melrose Plantation, the home of Marie Thérèse 'Coincoin,' a tenacious woman who planted the seed of hard work that grew into wealth and prestige for the future generations of the Metoyer family.

"The story of the Metoyer family began when Coincoin, a nickname her parents assigned her when she was very young, became Claude Thomas Pierre Metoyer's concubine. Born in 1742, Coincoin watched her enslaved parents treated horribly for sixteen years, and she made a huge promise to them before they died. She vowed to one day free herself from slavery and to make sure none of her children or their children down the line would be enslaved."

Sam led the group through the front doorway of the Metoyer home and pointed with a long stick toward a photo on the wall. "This here is Louis Juchereau de St. Denis. He was Coincoin's master. The story goes that St. Denis's wife fell gravely ill with an unknown illness. Doctors were summoned from all around, but none of them could slow the master's wife's decline. Her situation was so bad she even stopped opening her eyes. When she appeared to be on her last days, Coincoin stepped in and offered a concoction of African herbs and roots, a secret elixir passed down from her parents. The mysterious blend simmered in a pot for hours, and then it was cooled so the master's wife could drink the potion. Within an hour of drinking it, the master's wife's eyes opened, and within three hours she was sitting up and talking.

"Overwhelmed with gratitude, St. Denis gave Coincoin a piece of land and two slaves—a remarkable act, as it was the first time in the history of the South a slave had been granted such wealth by their master."

Karl spoke up. "Excuse me, Sam, how did that work? A slave owning slaves?"

"It's a strange scenario, right?" said Sam. "Coincoin was indeed made a slave owner but still remained a slave herself. She was the first slave to own slaves, but she still served her master, St. Denis, in addition to managing her property and overseeing her slaves."

What the . . . ? My mind was scrambling with questions, but I let Sam continue.

"While Coincoin took care of St. Denis's house and property by day, she managed her affairs and property at night, which included harvesting tobacco to get it ready to sell at the trading post each morning."

My mind flashed back to Lee's smoking habit and her early death. I wondered how long she might have lived if she'd never smoked. At least tobacco had first benefitted her family.

"This transaction in Coincoin's interest was the beginning of two hundred years of the Metoyer family's journey of expanding wealth. With the money she made from tobacco sales, Coincoin eventually acquired more than twelve thousand acres of land and hundreds of slaves."

How I wished Lee could have taken this tour. But wait, was it possible she *did* take this tour? She did know about her family's territories. Had she done a lot of research? Had she walked these floors?

My mind was buzzing, and at the same time I was completely content. The tour made me feel close to Lee again, and I knew there was nowhere else in the world I was supposed to be at that moment.

I listened with fascination as Sam told the group Coincoin had learned to hunt bears by spending hours hiding in the woods, observing, and calculating the animals' movements. When the moment was right, she thrust her spear with great precision. Then, with her slaves' help, she divided the bear carcasses into pieces and sold the hides and grease to European traders. Sam told us that one morning at the trading post, Coincoin caught the attention of a handsome young French merchant named Claude Thomas Pierre Metoyer, called Pierre by those who knew him, and before long Coincoin was Pierre's concubine. Meanwhile, her five enslaved children, whose father was also a slave belonging to St. Denis, stayed with St. Denis. Coincoin and Pierre's relationship blossomed into a twenty-five-year affair, resulting in the birth of ten Creole children.

Pierre was in love with Coincoin and wanted to marry her, but he needed his aristocratic family's approval, so he journeyed back to France to ask permission. His family said if he married that slave, they'd cut him off, so Pierre and Coincoin never married, but Pierre eventually bought Coincoin's freedom and granted her sixty-eight acres, including the land on which I stood at that very moment.

"What happened to their ten children?" Karl asked. "Did they remain enslaved?"

"No, they did not," said Sam. "Even though Pierre couldn't marry the woman he loved, he did everything he could to improve her quality of life, including emancipating all ten of their children. This process took many years—we don't know exactly how many—but in time they were all freed. And with

her own money, Coincoin bought the freedom of the five children she already had."

Sam explained that for the next two centuries, the Metoyers were the wealthiest family in the Natchitoches area. Their
homes had been decorated with exquisite furnishings, and
they'd had private tutors for their children and sent them to
prestigious universities. Many of the family members became
judges, priests, and mayors.

"But then the Metoyers' fortunes took a dramatic turn,"
Sam said.

My stomach dropped. Even though I'd daydreamed
through a lot of US history, I was married to a history buff, so I
knew what was coming.

"The Metoyers had long lived on land owned by France,
but as you learned in history class, in 1803 the United States
government bought up 828,000 square miles of the French-
owned land in a transaction called the Louisiana Purchase.
Because all of Natchitoches, Louisiana, and the New Cane
River territory, which had been owned by France, was now the
property of the United States, the Creole people lost everything their people had worked for spanning generations, so
you can imagine what happened to the Metoyers. If you want
to read all about it, there's a terrific book for sale in the gift shop
called *The Forgotten People*."

The tour ended, and everybody thanked Sam for a terrific
afternoon. Karl and I walked back to our car, and I kept shaking
my head, in awe of everything I'd learned that day. In just one
Internet search and one road trip, I felt I'd pulled the curtain
back on volumes about the mysterious history of my beloved

Lee. Now I understood why Lee felt such a deep connection to *Roots*. She was a descendant of a slave.

But even after a day of learning so much about Lee's people, I still felt I knew very little about Lee. And one fact nagged at me all the way home and for a very long time afterward: Lee's husband and child were missing from the family tree.

~~~ 16

By the spring of 2011, I'd been researching Lee's family for almost two years. After the trip to Louisiana, Karl and I returned home to Houston crackling with excitement about all we'd uncovered, and we decided that my next step should be to search for Lee's birth certificate by writing to Vital Records. But there was something wrong with the information I had on Lee because every letter came back stamped: *incorrect information supplied*. What incorrect information? What was I missing?

On weekdays, when I wasn't busy running our household and raising two kids, I wrote letters, made phone calls, and tried to come up with more ideas that might lead me to information about Lee's husband and son. Every effort led to another dead end. Many times, I thought it was time to give up. Even Karl, who had initially been so interested in the investigation, grew tired of my frustration. My kids made jokes to their friends while I was driving them to practices, "There's Mom, still trying to find where the bodies are buried!"

I was burning out, but I knew if I gave up, that would be the end of it all. My siblings were off living their lives, curious to hear progress reports now and then, but none of them were passionate about the subject. This undertaking would live or die with me.

One lovely spring morning, I took my two shih tzus, Zoey and Oreo, for a walk in Cattail Park near our home in The Woodlands. I sat quietly on a bench while my pets frolicked around the sprawling lawn of the dog park. Lee would have loved it here, I thought. She would have loved the warmth of Texas and the trees.

Across the park, I spotted my friend Vickie walking her two white terriers. It had been months since we'd seen each other, and I'd missed our lighthearted conversations about nothing in particular—weather, community gossip, and dogs, dogs, dogs. Vickie approached with the usual bounce in her step.

"Hey, Sandy! How are you?"

"Oh, I'm okay. You?" Apparently, I wasn't convincing.

"You're not yourself. What's up?"

"I don't want to bore you with my problems."

She smiled. "I'm no therapist, but you never know . . ."

Okay, why not, I thought. I hadn't talked to anyone about the quest in some time, so I let the whole story tumble from my lips, placing special emphasis on the fact that I'd tried absolutely everything I could think of and had hit nothing but dead ends. Vickie hung on every word, and after I finished, she said, "Lee needs to be put to rest with her loved ones."

She got it.

"One thing about truth," she said, looking out across the park, "is that it always finds its way out. You just don't know which route it wants to take until it does." Then, despite the fact that there wasn't another person within twenty yards of us,

Vickie leaned toward me and whispered, "I can help you find them."

Excited as I was by her interest and her offer, my mission fatigue had worn me way down. It must have been clear how little energy I had left because as I started to mumble gratitude that was surely tinged with a hint of "but you probably shouldn't bother," Vickie interrupted. "When you get home, send me everything you have on Lee. I'll let you know what I find out by tonight."

Was Vickie some kind of detective? It occurred to me I didn't know much about her. While other people at the park usually unloaded seemingly endless details of their chaotic lives, Vickie just smiled and listened. I wanted to ask her a bunch of questions about why she sounded so confident and why she thought she'd discover something significant as early as tonight. But I decided it was best to leave it alone. The less I knew right now, the more hopeful I'd allow myself to be. Maybe Vickie had astonishing research librarian skills. Maybe she was a triple secret investigator for the government or had spy training and wouldn't want me to pry. I left the park with a smile.

I spent the rest of the day doing just about anything to keep my mind occupied. I washed and folded the laundry. I swept and mopped the kitchen, then vacuumed all around the house. And I tried not to check my email every few minutes like a crazy person. Then, after dinner, I dashed to my computer, and there was a message from Vickie. With shaking hands, I clicked.

Dear Sandy,

I have found a person who matches your criteria, but not
your story of her life. Her name is Leaner M. Metoyer.
She was born in 1922 in Louisiana and lived with her parents in Chicago in 1930. Her father was Joseph Metoyer,
and her mother was Evelyn Simon Metoyer.

Are any of these names below familiar to you? Did
Lee ever mention the names of her siblings? Let me
know as soon as you can. If they are familiar, I will dig
deeper for their contact information.

Thx, Vickie

P.S. I found these names—Hazel, Andrew, Edwin, Gilbert, and Leaner Mae.

Already? I'd struggled with my research for two years, but
Vickie had dug up this information about Lee, her parents, and
her siblings in a day. My hands were still shaking as I typed.

Dear Vickie,

I think you're onto something! Those were her parents'
names from the Metoyer family record book. I remember Lee telling me she was the youngest of five and had a
sister named Hazel. Lee said they were all dead by 1965.
But wait, who is Leaner Mae? Was that Lee's name? Who
are you anyway, a private investigator or CIA? Just kidding LOL

OMG, Sandy

As I reread Vickie's email, my computer dinged.

Dear Sandy,

Below is the list of Lee's siblings, their birth dates and death dates, city and state, spouses, and telephone numbers. I think this information may be solid proof of her family, and I'm sorry to say her family wasn't deceased when she was living with your family. Now I'm as anxious as you are to learn more. Keep in mind that with this kind of thing, you can find yourself down a lot of rabbit holes, but I have a feeling we're headed in the right direction. I'm glad you asked me to help you.
Vickie

Hazel Rita, Born: 12/09/1911, Died: 06/05/1992
Chicago, IL
Spouse: Richard Player Sr.
No children
555-342-8900

Edwin Sr., Born: 11/12/1916, Died: 12/03/1963
Chicago, IL
Spouse: Lucretia Cloutier
7 children
555-678-9807

Andrew Joseph, Born: 11/16/1917 Denver, CO
Never married—Priest
No children
555-233-4501

Gilbert Bernard, Born: 02/09/1920, Died: 09/30/2005
Martinsville, VA
1st Spouse: Marie Hayden, 2nd Spouse: Barbara
1 child
555-340-9876

Leaner (Lena) Mae, Born: 09/04/22, Died:
10/20/1994
No number

Wait a minute. Not all of Lee's siblings were dead, even today? Edwin died in 1963, Hazel in 1992, and Gilbert died in 2005. After Andrew's name, there was no date of death. That meant he'd now be ninety-three years old. Lee had at least one living sibling! This was thrilling! But the emotional roller coaster I'd now been on for years kept rolling. It hurt my heart to think most of her siblings had been alive for many years while she was with our family.

In the next room, Karl was watching the Golf Channel. I screamed, "Honey! I found her family, and they're not all dead!"

"Great!" he answered. I could tell he hadn't taken his eyes off the screen.

I stood and started to pace the floor of my office, my mind scrambled with facts, clues, memories. I thought back to when I'd asked Lee, "Is Lee your real name or a nickname? Do you have a middle name?"

She'd said, "Lee is my name. That's it, just Lee."

And Vickie's email said that Leaner Mae was born in 1922. The year seemed right, but Lee had told us her birthday was

January 21. This document listed September 4 as her birthday. Why had Lee lied about her birthday? Or had she *not known* her birthday? Maybe Auntie Di had been right when she said Lee didn't seem like an Aquarius. Maybe she was a Virgo. I wasn't into astrology, but just for the heck of it I sat back down in front of the computer and looked up *qualities of a Virgo*. I read that Virgo is an earth sign and Virgos are known for practicality, precision, service, adaptability, and a multitude of talents. They're also prone to receptivity, sensitivity, and empathy—the very essence of the Lee I knew. But for thirty years, we celebrated her birthday in January. Why would Lee keep her real birth date a secret from our family? And why didn't she tell us her real name? Were those secrets somehow connected to her secrecy about her son and husband? And was it all connected to whatever she was hiding that she thought belonged in a book? I typed:

Dear Vickie,

I feel like a tsunami just hit me. I have so many questions. This must be her family, but I don't understand why Lee's family information isn't complete. Why isn't there any record of Lee's husband and son? All of Lee's siblings' spouses and children are listed with contact numbers. I wonder if she didn't legally marry the man in the military uniform. She never told me his name, but his name should be there if she married him. Maybe her son—she said his name was Pierre—was born out of wedlock and she was ashamed of it. I don't know. Something's missing. Things aren't adding up.

Thx, Sandy

Right there on my computer, I had the names of Lee's siblings, their spouses, and the number of children they'd had. Vickie's research had even listed their contact numbers. Why, *why*, had Lee never wanted to contact these people or to have them contact her? What had they done that was so awful she wouldn't even speak about them?

I turned the questions over and over, and then I felt another blast of adrenaline as I had a terrible thought: What if Lee's family had been searching for her all those years? What if they'd tried desperately to find their sister, to find out if she was alive, and all the time she'd been at our house hiding from the rest of the world? If I called and reached one of them, would they be furious?

I looked back at the list on my screen. Lee's siblings were arranged chronologically, from eldest to youngest. Gilbert had been the closest in age to Lee, so it made sense to me to start there.

With trembling fingers, I dialed the number.

17

The ring sounded strangely old-fashioned—both piercing and reverberating. I had to be calling a landline. After several rings, someone picked up.

"Hello?" said a woman with a soft, feminine voice. I guessed she might be in her sixties.

I bit my bottom lip. *Take a deep breath*, I thought.

"Hello?" the voice repeated.

Come on, Sandy. Pull yourself together. "Hello, my name is Sandy. I'm trying to reach the family of Lee Metoyer. Did you . . . did you happen to . . . know Lee?" My words stumbled, my voice trembled, and I could feel heat creeping up my face. I sensed I was crossing a line drawn many years before.

The woman replied, "May I ask who's calling?"

This was it. Out with it. "My name is Sandy Schnakenburg. Lee Metoyer was our housekeeper. She lived with our family for thirty years."

Silence from the other end of the phone.

I continued, "The reason I'm calling is my mother and Lee were extremely close until Lee's passing sixteen years ago, and my family has Lee's ashes. I'm trying to find the burial spots of

Lee's husband and son, so I can reunite her with her family. Do you happen to know where they were laid to rest?"

Doubts began to creep into my mind. Could my noble intentions be misconstrued as the behavior of a cemetery-obsessed lunatic? After an awkward pause, the woman spoke again. "Hello, Sandy, my name is Barbara. I'm the widow of Gilbert, Leaner Mae's brother. I must tell you, I don't think Lee was ever married. What I do know is that she had five children."

A sharp pain shot through my abdomen. *Five children. Five children.* The words echoed. Lee had five children.

I thought I must have called the wrong Metoyer family. That would explain it. This was all a misunderstanding. There was no way a good mother—and certainly not our Lee—would abandon five children to work for our family and never look back, not even once in thirty years. I could believe she hadn't married, but Lee had *one* child, the boy who died in the car accident. Nothing was making sense. All I could articulate was, "I'm sorry . . . what did you say?"

Barbara went on, "Ma'am, you should reach out to Ida Metoyer. I can give you her number. You see, I'm Gilbert's second wife. He passed away in 2005, and I don't know much about what transpired before I came into the picture. But if you contact Ida, she'll be able to help you. Ida is Pierre's cousin and presumably cousin to Lee's other estranged children. Ida is the daughter of Edwin, Lee's brother."

Pierre's cousin! The cousin of the child Lee lost in the car accident! This Barbara person had just called him by name. She didn't say, "the dead child's cousin." I tried to gather my scrambled thoughts. Could Pierre still be alive? That must be why I couldn't find his grave. My heart pounded harder against my chest, and I was suddenly full of hope.

"Thank you, Barbara," I said as I scrawled Ida's number on a Post-it note. Then a spongy weakness crept up my legs. Was I ready to know?

18

After the call with Barbara, I retreated to the routine of family life, immersing myself in carpooling, cooking, and cleaning, and all while thinking, *Five children. Five children.*

For six days, I avoided making the call to Ida as my thoughts swirled like a Midwestern funnel cloud. Too much of this story made no sense. I needed to know more. Then I decided, ready or not, it was time. *Breathe. Breathe. Long, deep breaths. Okay, here we go.*

I dialed.

When a woman answered, I cleared my throat and said, "Hello, may I please speak to Ida?"

"This is Ida," she replied firmly.

"Hello. My name is Sandy Schnakenburg—Barbara Metoyer recommended I contact you. I'm looking for information about a woman I used to know, Lee Metoyer. I believe her family name was Leaner Mae."

"Oh yes, Leaner Mae," she answered. Her voice sounded friendly, with a tinge of a southern accent. "Please excuse me for my ignorance, ma'am, but how do you know Ms. Leaner Mae?"

"Well, my family called her Lee. She came to us as a housekeeper years ago and eventually became a part of our family until she died in 1994. For some time now I've been searching for the gravesites of Lee's husband and son. She told us she lost them in an auto accident years ago. I'd very much like to lay Lee's ashes to rest in peace with her loved ones." I cleared my throat again and sipped from a glass of water.

"Her husband and son?" Ida asked.

"Yes, Barbara Metoyer said Lee was never married, but I find this very confusing because for all the years I knew Lee, she kept pictures of her husband and son on her dresser mirror next to her bed. Mrs. Metoyer also said Lee had five children, and this is the most confusing of all. Why would she have left them behind to work for my family and never even speak of them, her own children?"

"Ms. Sandy, Barbara was correct. Leaner Mae never married. I do know that she gave birth to some five children, but I'm not certain any of them ever knew her. They were taken away from her when they were babies."

I gasped. Again, I wondered if I had the wrong Metoyer family. But no. I knew these were Lee's people I'd found. "*Why* would someone take away Lee's babies? For the love of God—for a mother to lose her child, to lose *five* children? It's incomprehensible!"

Ida continued, "There's a lot to that story, Ms. Sandy. And the family has been searching for Leaner Mae for some forty years. We didn't know if she was still alive. My cousin, Pierre, got close once. He talked to a Chicago agency that did placement for domestic workers, and they told him she'd started working for a family in a northwest suburb. But the agency wouldn't give him the family's name."

Her words caused a hot, pricking sensation all over my skin. Now I felt like part of a conspiracy against Lee and her family. It *was* as if we'd kept her hidden all those years. How truly awful. I spat questions as fast as they popped into my mind. "Pierre is alive? So there was *no* dead child or husband? Pierre wasn't killed in a car accident?"

I wanted every racing question answered, and for no reason I could explain, I now felt I was up against a ticking clock. It was as if I'd just been offered access to a secret portal between the living and the dead and Ida offered the only path to information about what happened to the children, and to Lee. But before I could ask another question, Ida asked, "Ms. Sandy, would you like to know what happened to Leaner Mae? Before the family lost track of her, I mean?"

I braced myself. Of course, I wanted to know whatever there was to know about Lee. But Ida didn't ask if I wanted to know *about* Lee; she asked if I wanted to know *what happened to* Lee. I had a feeling I was about to hear something that would change my life.

Ida said, "Hold on a minute." I could hear her footsteps grow more distant as she walked away from the phone. Then I heard the footsteps heading back to the phone. She picked up the receiver and said, "This happened when Leaner Mae was eighteen years old. I'm going to start by reading a notice from the *Chicago Tribune* dated December 1940. I think you might want to sit down for this."

Why? *Why* did I need to sit down?

I could taste something bitter in my throat.

Breathe. Breathe.

Ida began to read. "An unidentified woman was found severely beaten early Saturday morning in Grant Park. Her condition is critical. If you have any information, please call the number below." Then she explained Lee's family had seen the notice, and because their daughter hadn't come home after work on Friday night and had now been missing for three days, they rushed to the hospital.

Of course, I knew what was coming. Of course, I knew she was about to tell me it was Lee who had been brutalized in a park. But she hadn't said that yet, so I was still engaged in magical thinking. Maybe Lee was going to show up later in the story. Maybe Lee was the first person to find the poor beaten girl. Lee had been a nurse, right? Maybe Lee saved that girl from death.

Ida went on. "So yes, Leaner Mae's parents linked the news story to their missing daughter. When they got to the hospital, they saw she'd been beaten so badly she was unrecognizable."

There it was. "Oh my God. Oh my God, Lee," I moaned, unable to hold back tears. It was as if I was hearing that Lee had just been beaten, now—in the present. Right then, I had an overwhelming feeling she was still with us and someone had just brutalized her, my beautiful, wonderful, gentle Lee. I tried to muffle the whimpering sounds making their way up from my throat.

"Are you alright?" Ida asked. "Should I say no more?"

"No, please," I said. "Please do. I need to know."

Ida continued, "Most of her teeth had been punched out. Her hands, feet, ankles, and hips were broken in multiple places. And the worst part was . . ." Ida paused, as if trying to choose her next words.

The *worst* part? There was more, and it was worse than this?

"She was found naked."

I closed my eyes and held my hand to my chest. I couldn't speak. I could only shake my head in horrified disbelief.

"The snow they found her in was drenched with blood, and from evidence around the scene of the attack, the police deduced there were multiple attackers. There were a lot of different boot prints in the snow, and the police could tell she fought back with all her might. The evidence showed that she drew blood from some of them. The doctors said she only survived because she'd been lying frozen in the snow all night, which slowed the bleeding. But her hands and feet were frostbitten. There was no trace of her clothes, purse, or ID. For three to four days, she was a Jane Doe."

I dropped the phone and shook my head in disbelief. Then I lifted my hand to my throat as if that gesture might halt my anguished words, my strangled sobs. But I didn't want to scare Ida off by reacting with hysteria, so I picked up the phone and said, "I need a moment. Please, don't hang up." Then I set the phone down, stepped into the next room, and let the tears flow. Oh my God, Lee. Wonderful, gentle Lee.

After a few minutes, I grabbed a tissue, blew my nose, and returned to the phone. In a flash of twisted logic, I thought asking something logistical might help me feel less sick to my stomach. My voice sounded suddenly frail. "Why was Lee in the park at night alone?"

Ida's voice was different now as well. She spoke more quietly as if it had just occurred to her that the news she was delivering was shocking, gruesome, and utterly horrifying. "She was in the park after her shift at a company on Michigan Avenue in Chicago. She always rode the bus home at night—the same routine every day. Her shift ended around ten o'clock, so she usually caught the ten-thirty bus home. She took a shortcut through Grant Park to catch it. She must have been followed on . . . that night."

Ida went on to describe more about the brutal attack and the aftermath, and like a fast-forward montage in a film, I pieced together aspects of Lee that now made sense—her false teeth, the odd way she stood, and the deformities of her hands and feet. I pictured paramedics scrambling around her naked body, wrapping her feet and hands—hard as ice—in blankets and warmers, blood dripping like icicles from her frozen lips.

I shook away the image. "Ida," I said, "what about Lee's five children? How did she have children after such a brutal attack?"

"About two months after the beating, Leaner was still recovering in the hospital when the doctors discovered in a blood test that she was pregnant."

"Oh, my Jesus."

Ida explained that even as Lee's physical wounds began to heal, she was still unable to speak or walk. And when she wasn't sedated, she'd wake up all through the night screaming with terror, uttering garbled words, clearly reacting to the trauma she'd endured in the park. Three months passed, and Lee remained in the hospital, incapacitated. In all that time she didn't speak even one coherent word.

She went on to tell me Lee's parents were facing their own personal health problems. Her father was suffering from liver cancer and her mother from breast cancer, so they were unable to take care of their daughter. Meanwhile, Lee's doctors said they just didn't know how to get through to her, so they made a difficult decision: for mental evaluation and treatment, she would be sent to Manteno State Hospital, an infamous asylum in Kankakee, Illinois, about sixty miles south of Chicago.

"How are you doing, Ms. Sandy?" Ida asked. "Shall I go on?"

"Yes. It's kind of you to ask."

"On August 6, 1941, six months after Leaner was admitted to Manteno State Hospital, Pierre Metoyer was born. Leaner was nineteen. Manteno patients weren't allowed to keep their children, so Leaner's family stepped in to care for baby Pierre. My father, Edwin, was Leaner's older brother, and he'd just recently married Lucretia, my mother. They agreed to take Pierre temporarily, believing it would be only until Leaner recovered."

"How truly awful for Lee," I said. "Her child—her first child—just taken from her."

Ida continued, "She wasn't the same person after the incident. The smallest trigger would terrify her, she kept having flashbacks, and most of the time she seemed lost in confusion."

"Was she speaking at the time of Pierre's birth?"

"No, she was still mumbling. There were no coherent words."

The idea of Lee not being able to utter coherent words made no sense to me. Lee had always been so articulate, such a lover of words. I asked, "Where are the other four children?"

"I'll get there," Ida said, "but first you should know that Leaner's mother, Evelyn, passed away in 1942, shortly after Pierre's birth. When Leaner heard the news about her mother's passing, she went into an uncontrollable screaming fit, further complicating her already fragile state. Meanwhile, she wasn't making progress, so the hospital staff tried an aggressive treatment called electroshock therapy, which they called ECT. After months of ECT sessions, she still couldn't utter a single coherent word."

"Ida, I'm trying to process all of this. May I call you back in a few minutes? I just need some time to take this all in."

"Yes, please do. I understand this is a lot," Ida said.

I hung up the phone, took off my glasses and set them on the table, then started sobbing and rubbing my temples. I got up to get a glass of water and tried to drink, but my mind drifted to the attack and Lee lying in the snow, freezing cold, naked, no one to help her. My stomach felt sick, so I chewed ginger to ease my nausea. Then I got up from my chair and decided to take a walk with the dogs before calling Ida back. I needed air. I needed to breathe, to try to understand where God had been during all that horror.

After the walk in the fresh air, I felt better, at least well enough to try to hear the rest of the story, so I made a cup of tea, picked up my phone, and hit redial.

"Hi, Ida, it's me, Sandy. Where did we leave off?"

"The Manteno staff recommended she be sent home for visits because the ECT treatments didn't stop Leaner's night terrors, nor did they help her speak."

"With her parents gone, whose home was she sent to?"

"Her first weekend home visit was at my parents' house. Neither I nor my five siblings had been born yet. The family introduced Leaner to Pierre as his aunt, and we think she knew Pierre was her son, but she didn't speak. She'd watch him constantly, playing and running around the house. She wouldn't take her eyes off him. My parents found Leaner's visits challenging. They didn't understand why she wasn't responding."

"But how could anyone expect her to be the same after such an atrocity?"

"They didn't understand the effects of the trauma, the emotional and psychological damage. They just knew she didn't communicate. It was as if they no longer knew who Leaner was inside her skin. You know—people can see only the external wounds."

I did know. I'd experienced that after my bike accident. *Of course*, I thought. This explained why Lee was so switched on about my internal needs after my accident.

I said, "Poor Lee. Poor, dear Lee."

"She'd visit on weekends and just sit in a chair by the front door and not get up from it. Not even to relieve herself. It became a real mess."

This image, in particular, was almost unfathomable to me. Tidy, proper Lee.

"The home visits to my parents' house increased to every weekend and became a burden, especially with my mother's brother, Paul, complicating matters. Paul had moved into their home after losing his job, and he had all the signs of depression. He slept all the time, didn't search for a new job, and didn't help Lucretia or Edwin around the house. He was just supposed to live there temporarily until he found a new job, but he wasn't showing any signs of leaving. During one of Leaner's home visits, she was left alone with him while my parents were out with Pierre at a doctor's appointment. Paul violently assaulted her, and Edwin and Lucretia returned to find her lying on the floor trembling in shock, so they rushed her back to Manteno. And if her being attacked again wasn't awful enough, weeks later they discovered she was pregnant again."

"Oh my God!" I shouted. "What did they do with Paul?"

"After Leaner was attacked, Paul was kicked out of their house, and he moved in with another sibling who couldn't support him, so he was forced to get a job and eventually move out to live on his own. I don't know what happened to him after that. No criminal charges, as far as I know. Then, on May 21, 1945, a beautiful baby girl was born at Manteno. Leaner named her Angel. But once again, Leaner had to give her up to another family member until she could be released from the asylum."

"Oh, Ida," I said. It seemed every step of this story was like another punch in the gut. But as Ida spoke, I listened and scribbled notes, afraid this might be our last conversation.

"Ida, do you mind my asking how you know all these details?"

"My mom and I were very close, and as I grew older, she shared everything with me."

"How did Lee's other three children come to be?" I asked.

Ida continued, "She became pregnant again. The next two children were a boy and a girl, fathered by an Italian man who held a prominent position at Manteno—I don't remember what that role was. But I was told Leaner was in love with him. Together they had a son, Tony, who was born in 1947, and a daughter, Serenity, who was born in 1949. Both children stayed at Manteno with Leaner until they turned one year old. It was against the rules to keep a child for more than a month, but because their father held a high position in the institution, he had the rules changed for Leaner. Tony and Serenity were then sent to foster homes until a family agreed to take them. I believe the father was married with his own family outside of the institution. He wasn't named on the children's birth certificates."

I felt rage. Sick, burning rage. I wanted to destroy this guy and burn down the hospital. "That institution should be sued!" I shouted.

"I agree. It's despicable. It's illegal. It's wrong on so many levels," Ida said.

Breathe. Breathe. Breathe. "Okay, back to the children. With Tony and Serenity, that's four. What happened to the fifth child?"

"The youngest child was Joey. He was cross-eyed when he was a toddler, and we don't know who his father was or who raised him. Perhaps he was sent to a foster home."

"Oh, the baby with the crossed eyes! I know about him. Lee had a photo on her dresser of a cross-eyed boy who she said was named Pierre. She said it was her son who died in a car crash. That must have been Joey."

"That's probably right; Pierre didn't have crossed eyes."

There was a long pause.

"Pardon the silence, Ida," I said, "I'm scribbling away here. I don't want to forget any of this."

"Of course," she said.

After I'd scrawled more notes, I asked, "Do you know what puzzles me most?"

"What's that?"

"It's how Lee could have bounced back from all this trauma. It's inconceivable. Even just *one* of the horrors you've described would be enough to break some people permanently. But Lee was a pillar of strength to our family. She was all positive. She was the kindest, wisest, most capable person I've ever known."

"That's called resilience," said Ida. "And yes, it's remarkable."

"I've witnessed resilience before, but this . . . Lee . . . it's another kind of remarkable."

"The Metoyers are known to be a very resilient people; their history speaks for itself," Ida said.

"Oh yes, I learned about Coincoin and her ancestors. What an incredible family!" I paused as questions crowded my mind, but what nagged me most was the idea that my family had kept Lee all to ourselves, that the remoteness of our home might have been part of the reason her children and siblings couldn't find her. "Ida, do you know where Lee's family thought she went after she left Manteno?"

"The Metoyer family thought she'd passed away after she left Manteno in 1953, thirteen years after she was committed by her parents, because no one ever heard from her again. Manteno told the family she'd been transferred to a halfway house, but Leaner instructed Manteno to keep her whereabouts confidential. No one knows why. It may be because of what happened at my parents' home with Paul. She was horribly violated there, and no one pressed charges. Leaner may not have felt safe around her family anymore."

I thought about that for a while. It made sense. Lee might have been looking for a safe place to start her life over, and with my family she felt that security.

"Lee was a remarkable survivor," I said. "Her story is as tragic as it is astonishing. Her survival, her transformation—they're nothing short of miraculous."

Ida sighed. "Absolutely. I think I've told you enough for now, and I know it's quite a lot to take in, but please call me anytime. I'm grateful we've connected. It's wonderful for me to know Leaner had a good life after all she went through."

"Ida, thank you so much for your time and honesty. I do have a lot of questions and will call you again. Just one last question before we hang up. Do you think it would be okay if I tried to contact Lee's children?"

"Absolutely," she said without hesitation. "I hope you can find them."

Ida gave me the names and approximate birth dates of Lee's children: Pierre, Angel, Tony, Serenity, and Joey. I knew I had to call Pierre first. In a strange, maybe even mystical way, I felt I'd known him all my life.

"I really don't know much about them, other than Pierre," Ida said, "but I bet they'd like to hear from someone their mother helped raise. It may give them peace to know that she lived out her life surrounded by a loving family."

For several weeks, I thought about everything I'd uncovered about Lee's past. What Ida had revealed left me saddled with pain, rage, and profound sadness. I needed time to come to terms with the reality of what Lee had endured and how she transformed into the person she was to our family. I needed to figure out if I dared to look even deeper into her past. Was *this* the story she wanted me to write? It was dark, sad, and so full of loss, I didn't think I could bring myself to share it with the world. And even if I could, I needed to find the meaning, to understand the hows and whys. I prayed for guidance, asking God to help me know how deep to dig and what to do with even more truth if I found it.

I decided to give Ida space too. She'd just shared quite a bit of very personal family information with a stranger, so I chose to leave her alone for a while. Then, after three months, I was ready to talk to her again. I wondered if she'd be willing to meet me in person. I wondered if she had Lee's birth certificate and whether I could see the article she had from the *Chicago Tribune*. I wanted to know if any of Lee's attackers were ever caught. I wanted to know more about Lee's parents.

With trembling fingers, I dialed Ida's number, but I reached only an answering machine. I left a message that day and several more over the next few months but received no replies, so I thought she might be sending me a message. I wondered if I'd pushed too far or had overstepped a boundary. Maybe Ida told other relatives she'd given me all that information and maybe that caused tension in the family. I decided to let Ida be and look in another direction.

I called Vickie and said I had a lot to tell her about the Lee Metoyer story. We planned to meet in the dog park later that week.

"You're not going to believe what I've learned thanks to your detective work," I told her. "Some of this is about as horrible as it gets, so bear with me as I try to retell it." I told her everything, pausing when I needed to take a deep breath or wipe my tears.

Vickie listened in silence, at times rubbing my shoulder or back as I spoke. "My God," she said after I'd finished. "I knew something really mysterious had gone on in Lee's background, but I never could have guessed. Oh, that poor, poor woman." We sat together in quiet for a moment, and then she said, "What a journey of discovery for you. How painful. How exhausted you must be."

"I am," I told her, "but I realize I'm only at the beginning. What I've learned has led to so many more questions."

"I'm here to help if I can," she said. Then she squeezed my shoulder. "But Sandy, take it slow. You need time to process the trauma of all this. It's as if you just heard all those gruesome things happened to your own mother."

For months, I was tormented by images of Lee in Manteno State Hospital. I lay awake picturing her thrashing and sweating as she hallucinated and experienced night terrors and was then tied down and zapped with electric devices. My stomach ached at the thought of her behind the walls of an institution where she was at her most vulnerable, a place where she was supposed to be cared for and rehabilitated but instead was impregnated *three additional times* after Pierre and Angel were born.

I found a therapist. My need to write Lee's story and my inability to move past the pain and confusion caused by what Ida had told me began to take over my life. Karl was relieved I sought outside help. He encouraged me to keep going, to keep asking questions, and I was grateful for his support and encouragement. I saw the therapist for only two sessions because she said if I just kept a journal and meditated, I'd be able to process my feelings and see my way to the other side of all this heartache. Clearly, I needed other sources of help.

I also started going to adoration at our local Catholic church, and during the silence of prayer, I found a sense of peace when I started focusing on the decades Lee had lived joyfully with our family. Was our family an answer to Lee's prayers? Or was Lee an answer to our prayers?

I knew this investigation I'd started wasn't finished. There was more I needed to find out about Lee's time in Manteno and more to learn about her children. And I knew I had to see this mental hospital for myself.

It wasn't long before Karl and I were in Chicago for a business function. Karl had to get back to Houston, but I delayed my return by one day so I could visit Manteno State Hospital.

In the lobby of our Chicago hotel, I kissed Karl goodbye. He said, "Good luck today. I hope you find more missing pieces. Be careful. This might be rough."

19

I got behind the wheel of a rental car and began driving south. For fifty miles, I thought about how many conversations I'd had with Lee over the years, how many hours we'd spent side by side cleaning or puzzling or puttering around the house. She was so content and calm, it never occurred to me there might have been violence and other horrors in her past. Lee's odd way of walking, her false teeth, and her vehement resistance to talking about anything personal had always made me curious about what she was hiding. But now that I'd been told about a woman who had been beaten senseless, who'd been raped, who couldn't speak or practice personal hygiene, who'd had five children taken from her, I found it nearly impossible to reconcile how the woman in that story could have been Lee.

When I entered the town of Manteno, I called the number I saw on a sign posted by the Manteno Chamber of Commerce and waited for the return call from Dick Balgeman, the person I'd been told knew so much about the inner workings of Manteno Hospital. Soon my phone rang.

"Hello, my name is Dick Balgeman. I'm returning your call from the Manteno Chamber of Commerce. What can I help you with?"

"Thank you so much for returning my call, Mr. Balgeman. Would you be able to give me information on Manteno State Hospital?"

"Happy to answer any questions you have." His sweet, sunny voice helped ease my anxious stomach.

"Fantastic! Do you have some time this afternoon?"

"Why don't you stop by my house around five and we can have some tea and talk."

Invited to his home? This certainly didn't seem like a guy who had anything to hide. He gave me his address, and we hung up.

I had a few hours before I needed to be at Dick's house, so I headed to the site that had been the home of the Manteno State Hospital.

As I approached the property, time seemed to slow down. There were miles of cornfields across the road from the entrance, and the enormous oak trees that lined the road leading to the hospital gates seemed to sway in slow motion. I pulled my car to the side of the entry driveway, stepped out to feel the grass under my feet, and stood in silence, taking in the freshness of the air, the peacefulness of all the green. In this quiet moment, I shifted my thoughts away from the images I'd been haunted by for so long, Lee beaten, bleeding, hallucinating, and terrified, and replaced them with pictures of Lee young and beautiful, sitting on a blanket on this sprawling lawn, bursting into one of her delightful fits of laughter.

Back when I learned Lee had been committed to Manteno State Hospital from 1940 to 1953, I visited my local library where I found volumes of dark, distressing tales of the hospital's history. I was so overwhelmed by the amount of information I found, I narrowed my search to focus on one woman, Genevieve "Gennie" Pilarski, who'd been a patient at Manteno State during the same period Lee was there. Because the patient records weren't kept private, books and the Internet revealed plenty about Gennie.

Within only a few years of each other, both Gennie and Lee were committed to the institution by their parents, Lee in 1940 and Gennie in 1944. Gennie was considered mentally coherent but unstable, which meant she showed intellectual competence but was psychologically volatile. Gennie suffered from episodes of manic-depressive illness, now known as bipolar disorder. And from what Ida told me, I inferred Lee had suffered from undiagnosed post-traumatic stress disorder (PTSD) and traumatic brain injury (TBI). Back then, little was known about how to manage these conditions, so apparently physicians at Manteno felt they had free rein to experiment on patients in an effort to find answers.

Gennie's parents sent her to Manteno because they were concerned about the manic episodes their daughter experienced while she was a student at the University of Illinois. At first, Gennie had adamantly resisted being sent to Manteno. At twenty-five, she'd already completed three years of college and didn't want her education interrupted. But she agreed to go along with her parents' wishes as long as she'd be allowed to return to school in the fall to finish work on her degree.

In one newspaper story I found, Gennie was described as a smart young lady who might have turned her study of chemistry into a serious profession. One physician noted Gennie was *neat, clean, tidy, extremely quiet but friendly and agreeable to her admission to Manteno. She cooperated with routines.* Later, he charted, *No signs of active pathology.* But it's also noted that as time went on, Gennie became a rambunctious patient the staff had difficulty controlling. Rather than release her to her parents' care, hospital staff subjected her to extensive experimental treatments, including an estimated forty insulin shock therapies and two hundred electroshock therapies.

Still a patient of Manteno in 1954, Gennie was placed in the "research ward," where she became a ward of the state. This was one year after Lee left Manteno. At the time, physicians from various Illinois universities who wanted to advance mental health research experimented on patients without their consent. Gennie was certainly one of those who didn't give consent, but it's likely her parents would have consented, presumably with little knowledge of what was occurring behind the hospital's doors. According to a *Chicago Tribune* article from February 18, 1955, when Gennie was thirty-six years old, she underwent a frontal lobotomy. The results were devastating. She was described afterward as *confused, unresponsive, and needing supervision because of wandering. Had to be led and helped. Unsuitable for further research.* I read that after the lobotomy that probably ended any hope of Gennie having a productive or independent life, she received seven more shock therapy treatments, but I could find nothing that explained the goals of those treatments. Gennie remained in a vegetative state.

For the next forty-five years, this once-intelligent woman was moved from ward to ward, then nursing home to nursing home, incoherent and incontinent. Gennie lived out the remainder of her life mute and unable to perform simple acts of personal hygiene. According to *The Neurocritic*, in 1999, at the age of eighty, Genevieve Pilarski died in a nursing home, having spent her last days *buried under her bedcovers, or roaming the halls of her nursing home, drooling and babbling.*

Today, the condition that landed Gennie in Manteno would be controlled by medication and cognitive therapy. Born at a different time, in a more informed and accepting era when people were speaking up about the rights of mental health patients, she might have lived a happy, independent life.

Gennie's story haunted me. During a time when I was struggling day and night to come to terms with Lee's past, I found Gennie's experience terrifying. If she had undergone such brutality and even torture at the hospital where Lee had lived for thirteen years, what had they done to Lee?

The legendary administration building where Gennie and Lee had been admitted into Manteno was now the location of a HomeStar Bank branch. I walked up to the iron bars that surrounded the bank and pulled on the gate, but it was locked, although I could see people working inside. Something about a bank being out in the middle of nowhere but still so heavily protected made me shiver. A woman inside saw me and got up from behind a desk, then walked to the entrance, unlocked the door to the lobby, and used a second key to unlock the gate.

She was middle-aged and wore her hair in a high ponytail. "May I help you?" she asked without inflection.

"Yes, is there anyone here who could give me information about this historic building, particularly when it was operating as Manteno State Hospital? Perhaps I could get a tour?"

I watched her face carefully as she considered my question. I wondered what she knew about the hospital's grim history. I wondered if she thought it odd to want to tour the place. She shook her head and said, "Sally would be the best person to show you around, but she's gone for the day. She'll be back tomorrow."

"I'm here only today. Would it be okay if I venture out on the property by myself?"

"Sure," she said brightly, "many people visit the grounds." Then she leaned in closer. "But I should warn you, a lot of those vacant buildings have remnants of the hospital's operations from way back in the day. It can be eerie out there, especially if you're alone."

My stomach surged. "Oh dear. Is there anything I should look out for?"

"Maybe a few ghosts," she said with a chuckle.

"Thanks for your help," I said as she held the door open for me to leave the building. What was I about to get myself into? The entire encounter with the woman, that strange bank— made me wish I'd talked Karl into coming with me. I thought, *Maybe I should try all this another time when I can have a proper tour. Maybe I should get out of here.*

But I lived in Texas. Seeing Manteno State Hospital with my own eyes wasn't a matter of a quick afternoon road trip. It might be ages before I had another chance. I owed this to Lee.

As I walked toward my car, I heard the click of the heavy lock behind me. Then, as if out of nowhere, a man in jeans and a white T-shirt half jogged toward me, calling, "Excuse me! Hold on a minute. You're looking for information about the hospital?"

It seemed he'd come from the bank, but the woman with the ponytail had just locked the door. This place was creeping me out.

He stopped a comfortable distance from me and said, "Hi, I'm Tom. I heard you might need some help having to do with the hospital. I know some of the history, and I have a few minutes. I was looking to stretch my legs anyway. Care to walk?"

I was in a public place, strange as it was, so I decided there would be no harm in strolling within view of a bank. "Happy to walk, and I appreciate the offer. I'm Sandy. How do you know about the hospital?"

"I've been within twenty miles of this place most of my life. You don't grow up around here without knowing something about big, bad Manteno State Hospital."

He pointed and began to walk toward the trees that lined the hospital's entrance. As Tom and I walked under the shade of the oak trees, he told me some things I already knew and some things I didn't. "Manteno started with over three thousand patients in 1940 and blew up to about eight and a half thousand by the time they closed it. Can you imagine that many mentally ill people in one place? That's more than ten times the size of my high school."

Interesting way to look at it, I thought. I told him, "Someone very dear to me was a patient there for about thirteen years. I wonder if she was released because the place was bursting at the seams."

"You bet it was. Beds lined up in hallways, no privacy, chaos."

"I don't know how deep your knowledge of this place goes, but I hope you don't mind my asking, do you know much about the pregnancies of some of the patients here? My friend was impregnated three times at Manteno, and it's my understanding a hospital employee fathered two of the kids. I find that appalling. No way the administration, the officials—whoever—didn't know what was going on. And to make it even worse, these women had their kids taken from them!"

Tom's voice grew more serious. "Yeah, I heard there was a lot of sexual abuse at Manteno back in the day. And some pretty awful experiments."

My head was full of everything I'd read about the experiments and Gennie, and I didn't feel like hearing more about it, but I didn't change the subject fast enough.

"During the war, they conducted malaria experiments. Shot patients up with the disease, killed hundreds of them." Tom pointed to a field across from Manteno's main entrance. "There's a mass burial over there. No names, just numbers." As I looked in the direction of where he had pointed, he said, "Well, I should get back. I hope you find what you're looking for."

I smiled. "Not quite sure what I'm looking for. I guess I'll just have to see what I find in those buildings."

"By yourself?" Tom's face contorted in surprise.

"No?"

"Well, I've heard stories about the 'abandoned buildings' too," he said, holding his fingers in air quotes.

"Um—"

"Nah, I'm sure you'll be fine. Just keep your wits about you. Nice meeting you, Sandy."

"You too, Tom," I said, and I could hear my voice sounded weak.

Tom walked back toward the mysterious HomeStar Bank, and I drove down a pothole-covered, asphalt road to the past.

The property truly was frozen in time. Decay and neglect were everywhere. It was as if all the patients were released or transferred and then everybody made a run for it, as if they were too spooked to stick around and clean up the place, to renovate and reuse it. I pulled up to a two-story brick building with several broken and boarded-up windows. The building was surrounded by overgrown grass and bushes growing wild. The hospital was closed in 1985, so by this time these buildings must have been vacant for over thirty years.

The second I stepped out from my car, I heard up-tempo big band music drifting from somewhere inside. Although I wasn't sure why—having had no connection to the military, current or historical—right away I pictured pin-curled dancers smiling big for lonely, revved-up soldiers who whistled and howled. The sound had the quality of an old radio. I walked to the entrance and pushed open the big wooden door, brownish red with peeling paint and thousands of scratch marks.

When I stepped into the enormous room just inside, I was overwhelmed by the staleness of the air. The windows up high were clouded with decades of soot, so thoroughly caked in black it was as if they'd been intentionally dirtied to obscure the view.

I could hear the music more clearly now, and I thought I made out Glenn Miller's "When That Man Is Dead and Gone," which my mother loved to dance to as she cooked. She'd swirl her hips to the beat while stirring a pot of spaghetti sauce and sometimes step away from the stove and twirl with picture-perfect footwork.

The music grew louder until it seemed to echo off the abandoned walls. The sound of it sent chills all over my back, shoulders, and arms.

I called out, "Is anyone here?"

No answer.

Though I hadn't moved from my original spot just beyond the front door, the music seemed to grow louder again.

Sweat slipped down my forehead, then down my neck as I became lightheaded from the thick heat. The air was dead in there. The sun tried to push through the filthy windows, and just enough light got through to send streaky beams through clouds of dust floating in the air.

I took small steps toward a shadowy stairwell across the room, staying alert to what was near me and what was in the distance. Several yards ahead, a broken wheelchair sat rusting. A decrepit bookshelf crumbled in the corner.

By the time I neared the stairs, I heard a different tune coming from the second floor. It was "Paper Doll" by the Mills Brothers, another forties song my mother had loved, this one about a guy who was giving up on love. Like the earlier tune, the music made me feel like I'd stepped into the past, and this song's slow opening cast a surreal moodiness across the room. Then the tempo picked up, which made my heart pound faster. It was as if I was being manipulated by some invisible music supervisor choosing songs for the film I was walking through.

Across the stairwell at eye level were hundreds of intricate spiderwebs, and tucked in the cracks along the wall lay clusters of hairy white buds, spider eggs anxious to hatch and scramble out into the world. I walked into a feathery light spiderweb and flailed my arms, trying to free myself from the sticky string.

Where on earth was the music coming from?

I took a few steps up the stairs and could have sworn I heard the deep voice of an elderly man. I couldn't make out words, only the tone—insistent, as if he was giving instructions.

I walked up the rest of the steps, and at the top of the stairwell a dark, dirty corridor led to a big wooden door with a huge crack in the center that ran the door's length, top to bottom. I walked to the door, eased it open, and peered into a room about the size of a big closet with nothing in it but a rusty desk, a wooden chair, and a dust-covered radio blaring from one end of the desk. I swallowed and turned my head in all directions. Where was the person who was controlling this radio? I could practically feel someone near me.

I said, "Excuse me, is anyone here?"

No answer.

Now I felt an overwhelming presence of someone else in the room, and I sensed I was being watched. But the entire building was silent except for the music and still except for the slow swirl of dust in the air.

I looked behind me. I looked up. I looked left and right. No matter how fast I whipped my head around, I felt the presence in whichever direction I wasn't looking.

My thundering heart told me there was danger in this building, so I turned around and bolted down the stairwell and across the main entrance and then gasped as I burst through the door and back out into the light.

I stood several yards from the building, looking back at it while trying to catch my breath. I still sensed someone was watching me.

I'd read countless articles claiming Manteno was among the most haunted places in the world, and I didn't tend to take such things seriously, but as I hustled to my car, I was filled with a buzzing sensation, as if my nerve endings were on high alert and telling me to *get away from here and do it fast.*

I threw my car into drive and sped away, thumping and bashing over potholes on the road past a set of mass graves marked with numbers, only glancing as I passed. I drove deeper into the property until I reached another of the hospital's original buildings, this one bigger than the one I'd just run from. It appeared to be one of the main medical structures and was now being used by a computer company. I parked the car, entered the building, and approached the receptionist's desk.

"Excuse me, I'm looking for someone who can tell me about this building back when it was Manteno State Hospital."

On the office wall was a black-and-white photograph of the hospital in 1950. In the photo, little cottages dotted the property.

A woman a few desks away stood up. "Hi, I'm Jillian. May I help you?"

"Yes, thank you. I'm writing a story about a patient who once lived here, a dear woman who was my second mother. Is it possible to tour this building?"

"I'm due for a break. I can show you around," she said brightly.

I followed Jillian as she walked through a doorway behind the receptionist's desk into a room packed floor to ceiling with boxes, then down a barren corridor and past what looked like an abandoned exam room with old medical equipment and something that appeared to be a dated x-ray machine and an old-style patient chair, all stacked up inside.

We continued down the hallway, and the farther we went from the lobby, the darker and more cobwebbed the building was. We turned a sharp corner, then walked to the top of a steep stairwell where Jillian paused, knelt, and pushed away two boxes and a table that blocked entry to the stairs. Then she began to step down into darkness so thick I could see nothing but crumbling cement steps at my feet and Jillian's dim outline as she descended farther and farther into the shadowy building.

I reached into my back pocket for my phone, and with my voice trembling, said, "Jillian, we need a flashlight." When I clicked it on, the air looked so thick with swirling dust, I didn't understand why we weren't coughing. After several more steps down, we entered a long, narrow corridor with low ceilings.

"What *is* this place?" I asked.

"This tunnel connected all the mental hospital buildings. It was used to secretly move patients, goods, and corpses throughout the institution."

Secretly? Why did it need to be done secretly? For some reason, I didn't ask her. Squinting through the darkness and decay, I tried to make out what was hanging from the wall ahead. I thought I was seeing black hooks, maybe made of iron.

"Are those cement hooks?" I asked.

"Yes," Jillian said. "The story is that these hooks, plus shackles, were used to chain unruly patients. It was one of many forms of punishment they used at Manteno."

Dear God, this place was straight out of a horror film. I restrained a gasp, afraid I might offend lost souls here in this abandoned mausoleum of dread. Jillian appeared completely unaffected by the creepiness around us. She seemed strangely cold, not even affected by the mass of dust particles floating in the air.

"Follow me." She headed deeper into the tunnel.

In a choked voice, I said, "Jillian, I think we should get the hell out of this tunnel. I'm getting a very bad feeling in here."

"Just a little farther," she said without emotion. "Sometimes I like to wander this place, imagining a patient passing through here. It brings the dead to life—"

Did I just hear what I thought I heard?

Then she said, "I don't often share with other people the heightened intuitive instincts that occasionally plague me in this building, but I can definitely feel some angry souls lingering."

This woman was completely freaking me out.

Then she added, "*Really* angry."

I took two slow, deep breaths, hoping to calm my heart rate.

"Are you up for seeing more?" she asked.

"Okay," I said, meek as a mouse.

I followed Jillian down another cold, stale cement hallway that led to a flight of stairs. At the top of the stairwell, we entered a small room full of more old medical devices that sprouted electric wires in all directions, making the machines look like some kind of mechanical Medusas. From the ceiling, old, rusty lights hung from electrical cords. A sign on the wall read: DANGEROUS. HIGH VOLTAGE AREA.

Oh God, I knew what this place was. I asked anyway. "What was this room used for?"

"It's where they performed the electroshock therapy. Zapped people with hundreds of volts." She shook her head. "Probably why they're still so angry."

I closed my eyes and imagined Lee gripping the bed, praying for an end to the jolting. I pressed my hand against my chest and shook my head. I had no words.

Jillian stepped over to one of the room's dirty gray windows and pointed. "You see that water tower over there? Behind that is a baseball diamond." Then she looked at me. "A baseball diamond built over an unmarked burial ground. That's where they dumped the bodies of patients who died from epidemics and from their creepy experiments, which were murders, more or less. Mass grave. Reminds you of Hitler, doesn't it?"

I turned back toward the door. I'd seen more than enough. "Jillian, can we leave now?"

"Sure. My break's over anyway. I hope you saw what you wanted to see. Here's my card if you have any more questions." She was as relaxed as someone just off a massage table.

I hurried to my car.

As I drove toward Dick Balgeman's house, I thought about what Lee must have gone through after she was released from Manteno and tried to rebuild her life after so many years in a place like that.

Her decision to no longer contact any of her family members and to never see her children again must have come with unimaginable weight. The woman I called my second mother was selfless, humble, and kind. I couldn't reconcile that person with someone who would turn her back on everyone who once loved her. But maybe she'd created her very structured routine, her clear likes and dislikes, her organized and regimented ways to serve as a boundary, to keep her within safely defined lines. Her habits, snacks, favorite meals, books, movies, crossword puzzles, jigsaw puzzles, her active commitment to the Chicago Cubs, and her love of Ernie Banks. It was almost as if she enveloped herself in activities and busyness to keep her mind fully occupied.

I thought about how secretive Lee must have had to be to land a housekeeping position with a family. What if she'd told the truth? *Housekeeper seeking employment, loves children, spent thirteen years in a mental asylum for severe PTSD, had a TBI, and suffers from amnesia as a result of a gang rape. Unable to raise her own five children due to her confinement, she hopes to make a new start, to join a family to help raise their children.* Who would have hired her? And what if they'd known she never intended to look for her children or communicate with anyone she'd known before today? How many 1960s suburban housewives would have entrusted their home and children to a woman who fit that description?

I probably would have judged her. I probably would have shaken my head and thought, *How? Why?*

Many times since learning the truth, I've asked myself what I would have done in Lee's circumstances. I genuinely can't imagine I wouldn't have scoured every millimeter of the earth to be reunited with a child of mine. I would have kept looking even after I had not a penny left, not an ounce of energy, barely any breath left in my lungs. So in trying to understand Lee's very different choices, I've been forced to look outside myself, to accept that the world is made up of countless types of people, people formed by unique childhoods, people who have untold assets and wounds and values and fears. I've come to accept that people can use only the tools they have.

I heard about Lee not looking for her five kids only *after* I'd gotten to know Lee herself. By the time I learned about her choices, I'd bonded with her deeply and extensively. I trusted her choices. Again and again, I'd seen her make strong, healthy decisions even under extremely stressful circumstances. Knowing Lee's altruistic nature, I guessed she decided she couldn't disrupt the children's stability at their vulnerable ages and was able to let go because she believed they were being cared for by competent, caring people. What was best for the children was what mattered to her. This was the Lee I knew.

As I pulled into the driveway of Dick's one-story, fifties-style home, I again felt as if I were going back in time. I rang the doorbell, and a silver-haired elderly man wearing a lightly wrinkled collared shirt and jeans swung the door open. In a wheelchair behind him sat a woman around his age.

I smiled and hoped my face looked calm rather than reflecting the frazzled afternoon I'd just spent being haunted by the ghosts of tortured souls. "Hello, I'm Sandy Schnakenburg, and it's a pleasure to meet you."

"Lovely to meet you. I'm Dick, and this is my wife, Susan. She has multiple sclerosis. Please feel free to make yourself comfortable in the living room here. I'll be right back." He disappeared into the kitchen, followed by his wife, and a few minutes later he returned with a tray holding a pot of tea and two thin teacups decorated with an assortment of flowers. Already I felt comforted. Dick and I settled ourselves in the living room.

I sat on a faded mustard-yellow couch covered in plastic, and Dick sat on an old Victorian-style chair. Like a reporter, I pulled a yellow notepad and pen from my bag and prepared to read through my list of questions.

"Thank you for having me, Dick. I have a lot of questions, so I hope you won't mind if I dive right in."

"Not at all."

"Thank you. First, can you tell me what your relationship is to Manteno State Hospital? I was wondering why the lady at the chamber of commerce recommended I speak with you."

Dick sat up straight, holding his teacup in one hand and gesturing with the other as he spoke. "I was the chief technology radiation specialist at Manteno State Hospital for thirty-five years, from 1948 to 1983."

Already I felt like I'd hit the jackpot. I was sitting with a man who'd worked at Manteno during at least five of the years

Lee had been a patient there. I couldn't imagine I'd have a better chance of getting close to what happened to her in that place.

He set his tea down and leaned forward as if he wanted to be ready to give my questions his full attention.

I asked, "What was an average day like as a radiation specialist at Manteno?"

"I worked in the Singer Building and x-rayed about a hundred fifty patients a day. The water supply would often get contaminated and cause widespread illnesses, so to avoid another outbreak, each patient had to be x-rayed every month."

"Wow. That's an extraordinary amount of radiation exposure."

"Yes, it was, but we didn't know the effects of radiation back then."

"How did the patients respond to that?"

"Most of them resisted being x-rayed, even though the machine didn't hurt them. I had to restrain them with straps because they thought they were going to get electroshock therapy."

The terrible image returned, Lee strapped down and thrashing. Then I shook it off. *Focus, Sandy. Act like a reporter.*

"The patients didn't trust the institution, which is easy to understand. They never got clear explanations about what was being done to them. They were just told where to go and what to do."

"Did they x-ray pregnant women as well?"

"Yes. Disease and infections spread like wildfire, so there were no exceptions. It was a time when doctors and staff weren't aware that radiation could affect the fetus," Dick said without flinching. I wondered how my next questions were going to sit with him.

"The male and female patients lived in separate buildings, is that right?"

"Yes, yes, they did."

"Do you know how it was that so many patients ended up pregnant at Manteno?"

I glanced at the photos on the table next to me, Dick with his wife and three kids.

If he was bothered by the question, he didn't show it. "Many patients ended up together in what we called the 'central park area,' the area between the male and female housing. Staff would supervise coed social activities, but during these events, many of the patients had sexual relations in window wells."

I found it strange that the staff knew this was going on and didn't do anything about it. Then I asked the question that had been bottled up in me for months.

"I read that doctors or staff sometimes had intimate relations with the patients and that so many unidentified, fatherless babies being born was one of the reasons Manteno was eventually closed. Do you know anything about that?" I really hoped this question wasn't going to signal the end of the conversation.

He shifted in his chair. "There were many unofficial claims of inappropriate sexual activities at Manteno, but nothing I can specifically recall."

"Were the babies delivered at Manteno State Hospital?"

He shook his head. "No, rarely was a baby delivered there. When pregnant patients were ready to deliver, the staff would send them over to St. Mary's Catholic Convent where unlicensed doctors delivered the babies. The mothers usually liked staying at the convent because they were treated so well, but the mother wouldn't be allowed to keep her baby for long."

I sipped from my teacup and tried not to think about all those innocent babies without their parents. All those babies separated from their mothers.

"The babies were offered to the immediate family of the patient. If that didn't work out, they were placed in an orphanage until the patient was released. Then the released patient could decide to either raise the child herself or put it up for adoption, but a patient couldn't decide this while still committed."

"It must have been horribly traumatic for mothers to have their babies just taken from them. I can't imagine anything so painful."

"Terrible. Very emotional. But it was the only solution we had. Babies simply weren't allowed to be raised in a mental hospital. The longest they stayed was one month unless there were exceptions."

Yes, I thought. *I've heard about two of the exceptions.*

Dick seemed like a decent man, so it was a struggle for me to hold back my frustration that he, like so many others, didn't try to stop what was happening to people like Lee.

I reminded myself to act like a reporter. "Do you know about the therapies administered to the patients? What worked and didn't work and whether there were any long-term side effects?"

"Well, some therapies led to unfortunate results. Of course, we learned that electroshock therapy severely damaged people's memories. And, unfortunately, all those x-rays I took eventually damaged patients' spinal cords, some rather severely."

"That's horrible! You must feel awful about the harm you did," I blurted out. Then I worried again I'd blown it. This nice man certainly couldn't be keen on being interrogated.

He answered as freely as he'd answered my other questions. "Not really," he said. "I was just doing my job, and at the time no one knew what kind of harm the x-rays caused people. Today, of course, we know a lot more, and modern machines are safer."

I thought about Lee's hunched back that curved more and more severely as the years passed. I wondered how many x-rays she'd been subjected to over thirteen years. Here I was, sitting with the man who subjected her to them.

"Manteno also administered hydrotherapy," he continued. "First, the nurses gave the patient a sedative so they could get them into the tubs. They strapped the person into extremely hot water and waited for them to stop screaming. When the patient finally calmed down, they'd unstrap them and immerse them in an ice-cold tub. This was a form of shock therapy intended to calm them down when they were out of control."

Lee and her aversion to baths. Of course. She was *so* relieved not to have a tub in her bathroom at our home. My God, I thought, the torture she underwent. It was even more excruciating to think she went through all that because she didn't come out of a vegetative state caused by a brutal rape.

As Dick continued, he seemed to gaze out the front window to the street or the trees, or maybe to the past. "If patients didn't respond successfully to these therapies, the staff took them to what was called the 'back ward' where uncooperative patients were punished. In the back ward, patients' hands and feet were bound with straps and chains. The patients were completely defenseless. They were highly medicated, making them virtual vegetables. As their medications wore off, the unbound patients would defecate on the floor and even tear off their clothes. Those people must have been terribly confused and scared so much of the time. Nurses would have to restrain them and place them in straitjackets." Dick pulled his sweater tighter around him. I watched his forehead pinch and his eyes grow sad.

I broke the silence. "What's the truth about these infamous tunnels?"

He turned to look at me. "Extreme cases were hoisted onto hooks on the tunnel walls, their feet and hands bound, to give them time out from the rest of the population. It happened when staff thought they had no other options, when a patient was too difficult to manage among the population."

"It all seems so inhumane to me. These mentally ill people were treated like animals, worse than animals."

Dick stood up. I guessed he didn't like my animal analogy. I didn't like it either, but I'd like to hear anyone dispute it. Most of what happened in that place would be a crime today. "Would you like more tea?" he asked.

"No, thank you. I'm fine."

"I'll be right back," he said, and then left the room.

While he was away, I decided to try harder to keep my anger to myself. As he settled back into his chair, he said, "We had some pretty bad epidemics back in those days. Flu, typhoid, tuberculosis." He shook his head. "A lot of people died and were buried in mass graves, marked with nothing more than a number." Again, he looked out the window.

I could feel he was beginning to grow tired, so I said, "Dick, thank you so much for sharing so much with me. I know this might not have been an easy subject to revisit."

He smiled, picked up a photo album from a side table, and handed it to me. "From the old days. Have a look."

I paged through the photos and spotted a picture of a group of patients in robes watching what appeared to be a baseball game on television. I squinted at the photo, hoping to find Lee in it. I didn't find her, but I wondered if the seeds of her love for baseball had been planted in that very room.

Dick asked, "I'm a bit curious. What has you so interested in what went on at Manteno?"

I wondered if he was going to ask that, and the invitation to talk about Lee made my heart light again.

"I knew one of the patients very well, Lee Metoyer. She was very special to my family. We only recently learned she'd been a patient here."

"When was Lee at Manteno?"

"About thirteen years, 1940 to 1953. Her niece told me that after Manteno, she was transferred to a halfway house in Fond du Lac, Wisconsin, where she lived until she was ready to integrate back into society. Ida said Lee had worked at a nursing home, and when I was young, Lee told me she'd been a nurse. She kept photos of a few elderly people in the top drawer of her bedroom dresser, and when I asked her who these people were, she said, 'They were my best friends.'"

Dick nodded. "Many patients who were in good standing were transferred to Fond du Lac. Manteno was in hot water because of the number of babies born there. There were allegations of sexual abuse and lots of suspicions from the surrounding community about what was going on inside."

I wondered about all those nurses and doctors and receptionists and janitors and administrators and all the other people who worked at Manteno and suspected or even knew what was going on but said nothing. I assumed Dick was one of them.

I checked my watch. I'd been there for more than an hour. "One more thing, Dick, if you don't mind. If I showed you a photo of Lee, do you think you might remember her?"

Dick tilted his head and said, "I'll sure try. I'm not so good with names, but I can usually remember a face."

I handed Dick my iPhone. "This is Lee in her full baseball attire at Wrigley Field before a Chicago Cubs game, radio and all."

He studied the photo. Then his face softened, and his eyes brightened. "I do recognize her. She was a sweet lady. She never gave us any problems."

I decided to believe that meant, "She wasn't subjected to the worst," and I took comfort in it. I slipped my notes into my purse, and we both stood. Then we shook hands, and I said, "It means a lot to me to learn all these things. I can't thank you enough."

"I'm truly glad to be of help, Sandy." He walked me to the door and waved goodbye as I drove away.
I drove to the airport thinking about everything I'd heard and seen that day. It was going to take time for me to process all of it. But I was overwhelmed with respect for what a survivor Lee was. She endured unthinkable brutality, violence, abuse, heartache, and loss but survived all of it and went on to create a wonderful life full of love and purpose. Lee Metoyer may have been the strongest person I've ever known.

Part Four

Spring

"Spring will come and so will happiness.
Hold on. Life will get warmer."

ANITA KRIZZAN

~~~~ 20

It had been a few months since I'd had the long conversation with Ida, and now I was ready to talk to Pierre, the man I'd always thought had died tragically in childhood. I prayed he'd take my call.

In my home office with the door closed, I settled myself at my desk. Then I picked up the receiver with shaking hands and dialed. After two long rings, someone picked up. "Hello," I heard a deep male voice say.

"Hello, may I speak to Pierre?"

"This is he."

"My name is Sandy Schnakenburg, and I believe the woman who raised me, Lee Metoyer, was your mother. Your cousin Ida gave me your number. I was so happy to learn that you're alive."

"I'm very much alive!" He laughed.

"That's the best news I've heard in a long time. I'm very grateful to be speaking to you now," I said.

"I thought my mama had passed away long ago."

Where was I going to start? There was so much to tell him. "I thought you had passed away years ago, too—as a young boy, in fact. I can't believe it's really you on this call right now.

All my life, I thought about you and how painful it must have been for Lee to have lost you in a tragic car accident."

"A car accident? Well, I'll be darned. Where on earth would you have gotten that idea?"

"It was your mother's story when she came to work for my family as our housekeeper. My mother requested a housekeeper who didn't have any family because she was hoping to find someone who'd want to become part of our family. The employment agency told my mother Lee had been hospitalized for shock after the loss of her husband and son in a tragic automobile accident."

"That's quite a story. She must have really wanted the job."

Pierre seemed lighthearted and was easy to talk to. What a relief. "Your mother wasn't the type to lie, so I think the agency was trying to help her get the job. The agency was required by law to tell a potential employer she'd been hospitalized, so I'm guessing they conjured up the story about the car accident. But now I see what they were doing, admitting she was hospitalized because she'd lived at Manteno for all those years. They obviously couldn't say that to a potential employer. Lee would never have gotten a job!" I could barely believe how quickly I'd jumped into telling Pierre all these things. I felt as if I was talking to someone I'd known for years.

Pierre said, "That was certainly conjured up. I was nearly grown up by the time she left Manteno. But no one knew exactly when she left or where she went after that. Who's the husband who supposedly died with me?"

I realized how jolting some of this information must have been for Pierre. But I was here to learn truth and offer truth, so I kept telling him what I knew. "Lee had a picture of a man in a flight uniform on her mirror for all thirty years she stayed with us. It sat next to a photo of a boy, toddler age, with crossed eyes. She said the boy's name was Pierre and that those were photos of the loved ones she'd lost in the tragedy. That's what I was told, and through the years my mother reminded me not to ask Lee about any of it because it was too painful for her to talk about. Mom said it might throw Lee back into shock, and she'd need to be hospitalized again."

Pierre was quiet for a moment. Then he said, "But Leaner was never married that I'm aware of, and that boy wasn't me. I didn't have crossed eyes."

"It must have been one of Lee's other children. Did you know any of them?"

"Not really, I met Angel but didn't see much of her. I don't know what happened to the other kids. I don't know how all these children came about while my mama was being rehabilitated at Manteno. It doesn't make sense to me."

"It's a miracle she got out of that place alive, and my family was so grateful for her."

Pierre was silent for a moment. Then he said, "She had a good life with your family, is that right?"

"She was the best thing that ever happened to our family, an extraordinary blessing. My siblings and I would love to tell you lots of stories about Lee. I can tell you one thing for sure: she was deeply loved to the end."

I thought back to my conversation with Ida and couldn't shake the image of Lee in a chair at her brother's house, just sitting there immobile. I pictured young Pierre crawling around her, just an innocent toddler playing near his real mama, whom he was told was his aunt. "Pierre, do you remember Lee?"

"You mean Leaner Mae? That was her real name."

"Yes, Leaner Mae," I said. Then I caught myself holding my breath. I didn't want to miss a word he said.

"The woman I called my mama all my life was really my aunt Lucretia. She was married to my uncle Edwin, Leaner's brother, who I called Papa. They raised me in the best of ways and gave me a lot of love and attention. When I was young, Mama told me Leaner was my aunt, but I learned much later in life she really was my biological mama. Mama told me Leaner wasn't well and had to stay in a hospital. But on some weekends when I was little, she'd stay with my family. She'd just sit in a chair by the front door and never move."

How awkward it must have been for a child to be around Lee when she was in the deepest recesses of her suffering. I decided to shift us away from the image of Lee at her worst. "I hope you don't mind my asking, but when did you learn Lee was your mother?"

There was a long pause, then Pierre cleared his throat. "When I signed up for the US Marines at eighteen. It was August 1959, and my mama gave me my birth certificate in an envelope. I was at the registry when I opened it. What I read completely shocked me. The worst part was that I had no father on the birth certificate. All those years of lies. I was so furious, I took all my paperwork and went home to confront my mama, Lucretia, and had a major meltdown. She consoled me, explaining I was a child of God, a miracle baby, and that being able to raise me as their own was the greatest privilege of her life. It took me time to get over it, and while I fumed, I decided rather than join the US Marines, I'd find my real mother, so I went on a quest."

Oh my God, I thought. This poor guy had been searching for his mother, and the entire time she'd been tucked away on our big property where no one could find her.

"I wanted to know my mother. I wanted to meet her and tell her I loved her. That's when I found out she'd been released from Manteno in 1953 and moved into a halfway house at Fond du Lac where, I was told, she gradually acclimated herself back into society. While in Fond du Lac, she worked at a nursing home for the elderly, and when she was ready to leave there, she moved to Chicago and applied for a job through a maid agency nearby. At the time she was living at the YMCA homeless shelter. I went to the agency, and they told me she'd been placed with a family on the North Side. I begged them to tell me where she was, but they couldn't give me the family's name. They were bound by confidentiality. I was devastated I'd hit a dead end."

I swallowed hard and began to tremble. I knew we were treading on fragile territory now. What if he could have found her, if someone at the agency had slipped him our name and address? What if Pierre had showed up on our doorstep asking for Lee? Would they have had a relationship? Or would Lee have denied him as her son to keep her alibi secure? Was there any scenario in which Lee and Pierre could have had a relationship while she was working for our family? I was heartsick that Pierre never had a chance to know Lee. But I had to accept that Lee didn't want to be found.

I didn't know if Pierre knew about the brutal attackers who had left Lee to die or if he knew how he'd been conceived, but I didn't bring it up. I wanted to do whatever I could do to help this lovely man who'd had so much taken from him. I couldn't go back in time to reunite him with his mother, but I could certainly help him see her through my eyes.

"Pierre," I said, "I'm so very sorry you didn't get to know your mother, but now you'll get to know her through us, my family, my five siblings and me. We have so many stories to share with you, we could fill entire days telling them. Your mother was the best thing that ever happened to us."

His voice was soft. "Is that right? That's wonderful."

Then I said, "We need a family reunion! My siblings and I want to meet you and the rest of Lee's children and for you all to meet us. We all loved her so much, and I know this might be odd to hear because you didn't know her, but for us, you're all that's left of her."

"I'd really like that."

I said, "I don't know if I'll be able to find her other children. Do you know where any of them live?"

"Where the others are is a mystery to me. But it will be wonderful if you can help find them because I'd like to meet them all. How about we all meet at my house in Chicago— everyone is welcome!"

"If I do find your siblings, I'll let them know we're planning a reunion at your house. How does that sound?"

"That sounds great to me. But I have a question about my mama. When did she die and how?"

"She passed away from lung cancer on October 20, 1994. My mother had her cremated and kept her ashes. When my mom passed away fifteen years later, we found Lee's ashes while emptying Mom's house. It was your mom's ashes that triggered me to search for you—well, really to search for your burial spot to reunite you with her. But now that I know you're alive, I think you should have her ashes."

In the silence, the heaviness of the subject seemed to hang over both of us. Finally, Pierre said, "Let me know when you want to get together."

"I'll be in touch, and we'll plan this reunion. So lovely talking to you, Pierre. I really look forward to our next conversation." He said goodbye, we hung up, and I just sat for a while, feeling a huge sense of relief and love for this man I'd still not met.

It would be over a month before I finished my search for all of Lee's children. Angel lived in Alsip, Illinois, only a few hours from Pierre's house. Pierre contacted her, and she agreed to meet us all at Pierre's home. I found Serenity, Lee's fourth child, Tony's sister. She lived in Shreveport, Louisiana, and was unable to meet at Pierre's house, so I planned to get together with her sometime near her home. I couldn't find any information about Joey, and I had no luck reaching Tony. I found the phone number of a Houston man with the same birth date as Tony and called the number. A woman answered and confirmed someone named Tony lived there, but after I told her Tony might be the son of Lee Metoyer, she hung up. Maybe the woman on the phone had raised Tony and didn't want the past creeping into their lives. It wasn't my intention to upset families, so I left it alone.

Soon afterward, Pierre set a date for our get together at his house on the South Side of Chicago, about an hour-and-a-half drive from Barrington. I flew in from Houston, and Barb came from Phoenix. We rented a car at O'Hare Airport and picked up Robin at her home outside Chicago. Roseann and Debbie couldn't join us, nor could Rob.

As we drove south on the 290 freeway, the sun's heat reflected off the dashboard. "Can you turn the air up?" asked Robin. "Hey, what if Pierre and Angel don't accept us?"

I twisted and tapped various controls on our rental car until cool air came blasting from the vent. "I think it's a good sign Pierre invited us over, don't you?"

"But they might think we kept their mother from them."

Barb said, "Lee came to us. We never knew she had living children. Maybe they'll be grateful Lee made a good life for herself and was loved."

I chewed my thumbnail. What if Pierre had taken time to think and started feeling resentment toward us, the people who had enjoyed Lee for so many years while he'd been deprived of her, his own mother?

Barb turned the car onto Stuart Avenue, where plush green trees cast shadows across beautifully manicured lawns. A group of children played hacky sack in the street. GPS said we'd arrived, and we all scanned the curb and mailboxes for the address.

"There it is!" Robin shouted, pointing to the right.

Barb parked the car, and the three of us got out and started up the front walk. Pierre's house had a New Orleans feel, with an elevated southern front porch and a swing; it reminded me of the Melrose Plantation.

The closer I got to Pierre's front door, the more I felt the significance of the situation we were entering. We were about to meet Lee's firstborn son and one of her daughters. This would be our first in-person connection with Lee's past.

My mind swirled with questions. Did Pierre or Angel look like Lee? Did they have any of her mannerisms? Did they drink their coffee black? Did either of them do that squinty thing Lee did with her eyes when she was skeptical? I wondered if they liked Irish coffee, baseball, caramel corn, and crossword puzzles.

I carried the urn holding Lee's ashes in a sturdy bag, intensely aware that each step was taking her closer to being reunited with her family. And there they were, Pierre; his wife, Vanessa; Angel; and Vanessa's sister, Doris, all of them waiting for us on the porch of the three-story home.

Pierre smiled and waved. Then he and his family stepped off the porch and walked toward us. When Pierre and I were finally face-to-face, I wrapped my arms around him. I couldn't imagine any other way to greet Lee's son.

With his warm puppy-dog eyes and wide nose, he looked just like Lee. I guessed he was in his late sixties or early seventies.

Right away I liked Vanessa. She had a sunny personality and a giant smile with sparkling white teeth. When Angel stepped forward, I looked at her and then at my sisters, whose wide-open eyes told me they were seeing what I was seeing. Angel was tall and had delicate hands and a smooth complexion—she was the spitting image of her mother. It was like standing in front of Lee again.

There were hugs all around, then Pierre said, "Whew! I never thought I'd see this day."

We all laughed.

I said, "I have something for you, Pierre. I'd like to give you the remains of your mother. She belongs with her first-born son." I handed him the heavy bag. He took a deep breath, smiled, and said, "Let's all go inside."

We followed him up the steps of a porch that wrapped halfway around the house. Inside, the home was beautifully decorated with beautiful wood tables, armoire, and chairs, and fine collectables. In the living room, Pierre removed Lee's urn from the box inside the bag I'd given him and placed it on the television. "I'm going to keep her right here, so I can keep a good eye on her. She won't be running away from me again," he said. Again, we all laughed.

We settled into seats in the living room, and Vanessa offered us something to drink. As we waited for her to return from the kitchen, my eye was drawn to a large framed photo of Martin Luther King and Coretta Scott King. It took me back to the day Lee watched King speak at Soldiers Field on television. She was so proud of the civil rights movement. It was because of Lee that I learned so much about what was going on out in the world.

The home had a pleasant warmth. It smelled crisp and clean, and I knew Lee would have been proud of her son's style, his tidy home, his grounded life. On the bookshelf sat a book called *Twelve Years a Slave*, and it made me think of Coincoin and all I'd learned about Lee's family's history.

I asked, "Have any of you visited the Melrose Plantation in Louisiana?"

"Oh yes, Vanessa and I visited a few years ago," said Pierre. "That was powerful. Made me proud to be a part of a family that had such a big impact in the South."

"Angel, have you been there?"

"Yes, I went many years ago, and it was fabulous learning about our ancestors. It appears our mom, Lee, definitely had Coincoin's strength and resilience!"

The weight of linking Coincoin to Lee carried us into silence for a few seconds.

Barb was the first to speak again. She looked from Pierre to Angel and asked, "Do you like crossword puzzles?"

Vanessa smiled. "When Pierre wasn't too busy during his shifts at the hospital where we both worked, he spent his time working crossword puzzles. He was so focused on the puzzles, he didn't notice me. I had a massive crush on him, and I kept trying to get him to notice me until one day he finally lifted his head and said hello. My heart melted." Vanessa giggled.

"Angel and Pierre, do either of you have an issue with spelling?" I asked.

"Oh, I used to! How did you guess?" Pierre answered.

Angel said, "I was a schoolteacher, and spelling was my biggest challenge."

I said, "Lee never went anywhere without her dictionary. Sounds like you both have something in common with her there. How about alcohol? Do you have a favorite drink?"

"Whiskey, without a doubt," Pierre said. Angel nodded.

I shook my head. "Incredible. Your mother's favorite drink was Irish coffee."

Angel was the quieter of the two. She seemed introspective and always paused before speaking. Her upright posture and hazel eyes reminded me so much of Lee, it was almost haunting. Around her neck hung a tiny silver cross, just like the one Lee wore.

"Did Lee have any religious affiliation?" she asked.

"She was a strict Catholic. She carried St. Jude's prayer in her pocket every day."

"I have so many questions," said Angel.

"I do too," added Pierre. "I want to know what Lee liked and didn't like. What was her personality like? What was she like with your family?" Before I could answer, he added, "Could you tell us a story about her?"

I wanted to tell Lee's children everything I could think of about their extraordinary mother. I knew it would take time, maybe even years to share all the memories and stories, and I vowed to jot notes in the coming months as things came back to me. For now, I would tell them a story that illustrated how strong Lee was, how ferocious and brave.

I looked at my sisters and began, "I'll never forget one time when I was eleven, and Lee, Rob, and I were the only ones home. Rob and I were playing catch in the foyer, and Lee was in the kitchen watching television when Rob and I saw an old beat-up Chevy pull up under the carport. I ran up the stairs to look out the window. The guy getting out of the car didn't see me. He had something metal in his hand, and he walked in a creepy slow-motion way, right up to the front door where he started picking the lock. I ran back downstairs and told Lee someone was trying to break in, that the knob on the front door was wiggling."

Pierre, Angel, Vanessa, and Doris leaned forward, as if trying to get closer to the story.

"Lee grabbed a broom from the kitchen utility closet and ordered Rob and me to hide around the corner near the powder room, but we peeked around the corner and watched

everything. Lee jerked the door open and screamed at the bur-
glars, 'Hey!' Then she pointed the broom like a bayonet. The
guy dropped a wire hanger on the porch and sprinted to his
car. As he took off, Lee shouted all kinds of threats and swear
words Robbie and I knew we weren't supposed to hear, and we
watched in awe from our hiding place."

At the mention of Lee's swearing, Pierre laughed.

"But that's not even the craziest part! Lee didn't slam the
door, lock up the house, and call the police. She ran after the
guy. Rob and I had run halfway up the stairs to watch from a
window, and we saw the wannabe burglar jump into his car and
start to peel off down the driveway as Lee ran after him, with
her awkward gait, waving her broom. Then she launched it into
the air like a javelin, and *BAM!* It hit the trunk of the guy's car
as he sped away."

By now everyone in the room was laughing.

"It was like watching a scene in a superhero movie. Lee was
fearless. When she walked back into the room—after retriev-
ing the broom, of course—she was shaking. Rob and I just
stood there, staring. I gushed at her, 'You chased off a burglar
with a broom!' Her bravery was off the charts."

"That was Lee," added Robin. "Extraordinary courage, and
it wasn't as if she was bulky and strong. She was an elegantly tall
woman and about forty-seven years old at the time."

Pierre, Angel, Vanessa, and Doris's faces were glowing,
their smiles bright and wide. I added, "And for the record, our
house was the only home on Rainbow Road that was never
robbed."

Barb said, "I remember how consistent Lee was. As one
of the first members of the Chicago Cubs Die-Hard Cub Fan

Club, she never wavered from her dedication to baseball. Over the years, a lot of things changed in our family, but one thing that stayed the same year after year was Lee's dedication to the Cubs. For Christmas, she always wanted whiskey, puzzles, books, peanut brittle, or anything having to do with the Cubs."

Robin said, "She also loved playing Scrabble with Mom, Auntie Di, and Grandma. And she *loved* putting puzzles together..."

I thought back to all the times I'd acted as Lee's chauffeur. "I remember when Lee would ask me to drive her to BJ's liquor store to buy whiskey and a carton of Pall Malls. Sometimes we'd go to dinner at her favorite restaurant, Red Lobster."

Robin laughed. "And she was obsessed with Cracker Jacks, Harlequin romance novels, classic movies, cornbread, and baby back barbeque ribs."

"I can tell you what she didn't like," Barb said. "Our dogs. One winter, Pudgy knocked her into the in-ground garbage can, and Lee broke her leg. Lee also wouldn't get near our pool. She was terrified of water."

I tried not to wince whenever someone shared a memory that pointed back to the terrible things that had happened to Lee. I did my best to focus on the wonder of this glorious day.

By the time dusk began to seep through the open windows, we realized we'd been there most of the afternoon. Pierre said, "It gives me real peace to know my mother lived out her later years so well loved. And it means a lot that you're here with us now. It's a testament to what a great mother she was to you."

I closed my eyes, overwhelmed by the sincere kindness of this man. My heart was full. I said, "It may be a good time to give you your gifts." Pierre's family's eyes lit up with surprise.

Barb reached over to the big bag next to her chair and pulled out two custom-made memory books we'd put together. It was a photo essay that included every picture we had of Lee. She said, "We've made copies for you both and a copy for Serenity."

"Oh my, I didn't expect such a beautiful gift," Angel said.

Pierre's and Angel's eyes welled up as they turned the pages. Photo after photo showed their mother smiling and laughing. Lee at the baseball game with her radio, Lee at the sink with that skeptical look I remember so vividly, Lee at Christmastime surrounded by Krilich grandchildren. My stomach fluttered when I saw the photo of Lee in her white uniform, taken during one of her first days at Rainbow Road.

As Pierre and Angel turned page after page, my sisters and I watched their faces change—from smiles to squinted eyes that seemed to be fighting tears and to smiles again. Now and then Robin, Barb, and I added a thought, an anecdote, a memory.

I looked at the grandfather clock in the corner, then glanced at Barb and nodded toward the door. It was time to leave Lee's children alone with their thoughts.

We headed toward the front door, passing a family photo on a table. It was of a beautiful girl dressed in a red dress, her hair done up perfectly as if she was going to a dance. "Is this one of Lee's grandchildren?" I asked.

"Yes, it is," Vanessa said, smiling. "And now I know how much she looks like her grandmother."

How wonderful, I thought, the idea of Lee's bloodline already continuing on in her grandchildren. What a magnificent grandmother she would have been to that little girl.

We all walked outside together, and when we reached the car, Pierre said, "My daughter is getting married in a few months, and you're all invited. Perhaps we can sing 'We Are Family' together!" He threw his head back in laughter, and we all laughed with him.

"We'd love to come," I said.

"Love to," agreed Robin.

"Absolutely and thank you!" said Barb.

Just before getting into the car, I remembered I had two more gifts for Pierre and Angel. I reached into the back seat, then handed them two Bibles, both tattered and old. Tucked inside each Bible was a small card of St. Jude's prayer. "Lee faithfully kept this prayer in her pocket every day. I know she'd want you two to have them."

Angel hugged each of us. "Oh, this is beautiful. Thank you so much for giving me something that was so dear to my mother."

"I'll keep her Bible right next to my bed. Thank you so much," Pierre said.

I reached for the car door, then turned back. "Pierre, I think you should know Lee had a final request. She said if the Cubs won the World Series in our lifetime, she wanted a teeny bit of her ashes to be sprinkled on Wrigley Field, the place she loved most in the world."

"We might be waiting a long time, but if it ever happens, consider her wish granted!" Pierre said.

The seven of us exchanged more hugs, then my sisters and I settled into the car, and we all waved and blew kisses until the wonderful members of Lee's family were no longer in sight.

~~~ 21

Wishing a championship for the Chicago Cubs was like hoping Halley's Comet would blast through the sky alongside Santa Claus. Year after year, my family loyally watched Cubs games hoping *this* would be the year they'd win the World Series. And every year, like all Cubs fans, we'd have our hearts broken. By the time Lee passed away in 1994, the Cubs were in year eighty-six of a miserable losing drought, so her beloved team didn't take the title in her lifetime.

But I kept hoping, kept praying, kept watching. Lee had spent thirty miraculous minutes on the phone with Chicago's own Ernie Banks, and now I wanted nothing more than for her cherished team to win the World Series so some of her ashes could be scattered on Wrigley Field. With that, I'd fulfill one of Lee's greatest dreams. So for twenty-one years after her death, I dutifully watched the Cubs from April to September only to see them end every season without a World Series win. They won the National Central Division title in 2003, 2007, and 2008. But not the World Series.

Then came 2016.

In 2016, the Chicago Cubs made it to the World Series for the first time since 1945. It had now been 108 years since they'd won a World Series, and as they went into combat against the Cleveland Indians, the city of Chicago was ecstatic with hope.

The series was excruciating. Cleveland won the first two games, which caused Cubs fans to glumly prepare to have their hearts broken yet again. Then Chicago won the next three, and the city once again pulsed with hope that a Commissioner's Trophy would be awarded to their beloved team for the first time in more than a century. Then the Indians took game six, so it all came down to game seven.

I watched game seven in Texas, surrounded by a room full of friends and with Karl by my side. At the top of the eighth inning, Chicago was ahead 6–3, and to stop gnawing my nails, I started chewing ice.

Then came the bottom of the eighth. Cleveland scored three runs, and when they tied the game, I screamed, "Noooo!" so loud my dogs started howling.

Nobody scored in the ninth, and at the top of the tenth, rain gushed from the sky. I grabbed a throw pillow, pressed it into my face, and screamed into it. This game could *not* be rained out. I couldn't take another day of this.

Mercifully, the rain came and went, delaying the game for about fifteen minutes, and it was game on again. Ben Zobrist hit a go-ahead double, and Miguel Montero sent him home with an RBI. The Cubs were now up by two, which launched the Chicago crowd into a frenzy, jumping up and down, cheering, waving Cubs towels and hats.

Then it was the bottom of the tenth. The Indians had two outs, and when Michael Martinez grounded out to third, that was it. It was all over. The Chicago Cubs had broken their losing streak and clinched the World Series!

All across Chicago, fans dressed in blue, red, and white poured into the streets as the city exploded into an enormous dancing, drinking, screaming party. Around the city, people cried and sang and hugged strangers. It was a glorious event, and I got to see it happen. After the last out, I walked outside, looked up at the sky, and said, "Lee, they did it! Congratulations, dear friend." It was Lee's magic moment, and she had the best seat in the house.

After the big win, I opened my Facebook account to see countless relatives and friends had posted excited comments about how much Lee had longed for this day. People from all over the country called to share their joy that Lee's team had finally done it, had broken the curse. And almost all of them said they just knew Lee was watching it all from heaven.

Now all we had left to do was find a stealthy way to sprinkle a few ashes on Wrigley Field, a field so famous for the tradition it was eventually outlawed. I had a feeling we'd find a way.

$\mathscr{mathscr}$ **22**

In time, I learned why Ida hadn't returned my calls. Tragedy had once again struck the Metoyer family. A few weeks after our conversation, Ida was diagnosed with stage four brain cancer and died within weeks. I'd left several messages, but I imagine her husband was so grief-stricken the last thing he wanted to do was help some stranger sift through dark family secrets.

I'd given up trying to connect with Lee's sons Tony and Joey. But not long after the Cubs victory, my sister Barb flew in from Phoenix and we set out on another road trip, this time to Shreveport, Louisiana, where we planned to meet Lee's daughter Serenity. Despite a Texas thunderstorm that launched raindrops as big as autumn grapes onto our windshield, we weren't about to reschedule. I gripped the steering wheel tight and didn't relax until we pulled into the Cracker Barrel parking lot.

As we walked into the restaurant, I said to my sister, "I forgot to ask Serenity what she looks like."

We stood at the hostess stand, scanning the room for someone who looked like Lee. Barb said, "Maybe we should walk around?"

We wandered through the restaurant trying not to seem invasive as we tried to sneak a good look at the faces of the diners. In one booth, a man and a woman sat next to each other, and the woman caught my eye. She didn't look like Lee, but I could tell they were both looking for someone.

I walked up to their booth and said to the woman, "Would you by any chance be Serenity?"

"Yes," the woman replied in a high-pitched voice. "That would make you Sandy and Barb?"

Serenity had beautiful big eyes, fair velvety skin, and lovely brown curly hair. She wore a bright purple blouse and a smile that practically stretched beyond the width of her face. She was a beautiful woman, but I sensed a heaviness. We hugged hello, and she said, "I'd like you to meet my husband, Phil."

Phil's hair was gray, and his eyes were kind and gentle. The two of them were cuddly and seemed very much in love.

"Lovely to meet you both," Barb and I said almost in sync.

The waitress arrived to take our orders, but we asked for more time so we could get acquainted. I let out a satisfied sigh. "Serenity, it is so nice to finally meet you. You're just beautiful, and your eyes, so big and bright."

"You're too kind. I was told I don't look much like my mother. Do you agree?"

"I would agree. You must have taken after your father. Do you know what he looked like?" I knew I was treading into dangerous territory. If she was troubled by my question, she didn't show it.

"Ida said my father was an Italian man employed at Manteno State Hospital and that he may have had a family of his own. I don't know anything about him, not even his name. Ida told me he was in love with my mother for a long time. I'm not sure how she knew that."

Barb's eyes nearly popped out of her head. "Lee in love? We never heard Lee use such words. But maybe she was a secret romantic. Maybe that's why she read all those Harlequin romance novels."

I thought about how horrible it must have been for Lee to have loved a married man and to have had children with him, always knowing she'd probably never be able to have a life with him.

Serenity continued, "I also have a full-blooded brother, Tony, born in 1947, two years before me."

"Have you ever met him?" I asked.

"Only once. My mother who raised me was going to raise him, too, but changed her mind." Her eyes turned sad. "I would have loved having a brother."

"I'm so sorry that happened," said Barb. "I bet he would have loved having a sister."

The waitress returned to our table, and this time we ordered. Then Serenity cleared her throat, peered into her purse, pulled out two photos, and placed them on the table. One picture was of Lee as a young woman holding a little girl about a year old in her arms. Right away I realized the photo had been taken on the front lawn at Manteno.

"Tony and I were two years apart, and we were allowed to stay with our real mother, Leaner, at Manteno for the first year of our lives. Leaner had named me Violet, but when my new mother decided to keep me, she changed my name to Serenity."

"What happened to Tony?" I asked.

"When he was a year old, he was placed in an orphanage waiting for Leaner's release. But by the time he was eight, Leaner still hadn't come for him, so they contacted my new mother to see if she wanted to raise him. She and I went down to the orphanage somewhere in Chicago. My mother asked if I wanted a brother, and I squealed, 'Yes, yes!' But after we met him, she decided she didn't want to raise another child. I don't know why. I cried for days."

Phil rubbed her shoulder but stayed silent. Throughout the lunch, he'd let her do the talking and remained quietly supportive by her side. Serenity continued, "At the time, I didn't know he actually was my brother. And I can't imagine what kind of pain he must have felt if he knew we were there to adopt him but left the orphanage without him. I never saw him again. I don't know what became of him but still think about him all the time."

This wouldn't be the first time I had no words. I imagined Lee overwhelmed with grief over losing both of her children after being able to mother them for their first year. I pictured both children crying for her as they were taken away.

"The woman who raised me was a friend of the Metoyer family. I'm not sure how she was connected, exactly, and I was never legally adopted," Serenity said with a frown.

"Is this hard to talk about?" Barb asked.

"Yes," Serenity said with a shaky voice. "She was callous. She accused me of being crazy 'like your real mother,' she'd say. She didn't really like children."

"I'm so sorry that happened to you," I said.

I calculated Serenity's age at about sixteen when Lee arrived at our home in 1965. Lee must have made a choice to not disrupt her stability. I believe she was thinking of what was best for her daughter, but as I thought about it now, I felt awful. I wanted to reach back in time, yank Serenity out of that miserable situation and bring her to live with us.

Our lunches were served, but I had little appetite. I wanted to tell Serenity all about what an extraordinary lady her biological mother had been and to make clear she certainly had not been crazy. But I was also afraid of causing her more pain, so I treaded gently as I told her a few stories that illustrated what a gift her mother was to our family. She seemed sincerely happy her mother had found joy in the last thirty years of her life.

After lunch, Barb handed Serenity a copy of the photo book we'd given Pierre and Angel. Serenity slowly turned each page, stopping to study every picture of Lee. It was the happiest I'd seen her since we met. She said, "It's wonderful that my mother was so loved by your family."

"She definitely was," I said. "I hope knowing that gives you peace. I think it helped Pierre and Angel. And I hope someday you can spend time with them. They're wonderful people."

"I hope so too, but I don't travel much anymore," Serenity said.

There was a pause in the room, then Barb asked, "Serenity, do you have any children?"

"Yes, I have one son, Jesus. He's a handsome man. Let me show you a picture."

Serenity pulled out a photo of her son, and I gasped. "He looks just like Lee!"

"Yes, I can see that now as I look through these photos. That gives me comfort."

The rain had let up, and the four of us headed out of the restaurant. While standing in the parking lot, we snapped a few photos together, said our goodbyes, and went our separate ways.

As we drove, Barb and I talked about Serenity and Lee, Pierre and Angel, Lee's kids we didn't find, Melrose Plantation, Manteno State Hospital, Mom, Dad, and Rainbow Road. We talked about how painful it was to know Lee had children who for years wondered about her and desperately looked for her while she was tucked away in Barrington, hovering over us. We shared story after story beginning with, "Remember that time . . ." and "Can you believe . . ." and some that ended with, "I'm so glad those days are behind us."

Then my sister and I went quiet. She focused on the road as I watched the high clouds begin to clear and thought about what a force Lee had been in my life, how her every action had been marked with love and kindness. Because of Lee, my childhood had been an embarrassment of emotional riches. I'd had two mothers, both of whom showered me with patience and genuine care.

Soothed by the rumble of the road beneath me, I tried to take in the enormity of everything I'd learned by digging into Lee's past, the people I'd met, the places I'd seen. I felt as if I'd just left a theater after watching a movie so powerful I knew it would never let go of me.

I'd done it. I'd uncovered Lee's big secret. I'd finally found out the truth, many truths, behind the subject we'd been told never to ask about, Lee's secret past. In all my prying and hinting and digging throughout my childhood and into young adulthood, not once did it occur to me she might have been the victim of savage crimes. Never could I have imagined my lighthearted, even-tempered, peaceful second mother had been beaten, raped, left for dead, terrorized, hospitalized, and rendered temporarily helpless. If I'd ever had reason to imagine the life of someone years after experiencing the kinds of brutality Lee did, I never would have pictured a content, soft-spoken, protective, wise person who could find sweet happiness in something as simple as a baseball broadcast or a jigsaw puzzle. Before learning the secret of Lee's past, I had no genuine understanding of the strength of the human spirit.

Do we ever really get over the severe wrongs done to us, the worst of the wounds inflicted on us? How do we know if we're healed, if we're even capable of completely healing? In Stephanie Foo's memoir, *What My Bones Know*, she writes that her then-boyfriend, Joey, told her, "It's okay to have some things you just can't get over." With that one simple thought, he gave her something no one ever had: acceptance of the complex and miraculous and sometimes troubled woman she'd become both despite and because of her damaging past.

I wondered if anyone gave Lee that kind of gift, the freedom to dismiss parts of the past, to embrace other parts, to use whichever parts she chose to use however she might use them. Or did she give that gift to herself? Did Lee find her own way to some miraculous acceptance of her past, and was she therefore able to step away from its menacing shadow?

Barb and I were still on the road when the sun sank low in the sky. I turned to my sister and caught her eye, and she gave me a silent smile that said she understood. I leaned my head against the glass, looked out across the flaming orange sky in the west, and thought, *I see you, Lee. I see you out there. And guess what, I worked the puzzle you left me.*

I love how Lee loved puzzles. She loved how they offered time for quiet contemplation. And she saw a world of life lessons within a puzzle's metaphors. By asking me to write her story, Lee knew she was handing me the greatest puzzle of my life. And I think she knew that in the process of unearthing her past and crafting a story from it, I'd be forced to tiptoe through the minefield of my own past.

Lee knew me, really knew me. She knew what I feared, she knew what I needed, and she knew what I'm capable of—long before I ever did. I think she knew if she assigned me this intricate and distressing and at times even dangerous puzzle, I'd work all the way through it, starting by dumping all the pieces on the table and flipping them over one by one, then building the frame. Lee knew I'd complete the task for her; did she also know I'd figure out why she'd assigned it to me? How could she not? She was part Dear Abby, part Sigmund Freud, part Mary Poppins, part Maria von Trapp. She was grace and empathy, insight and intelligence, all laced with magic. Now and then she was even muscle. Lee was everything.

For her last act, she handed me a ten-thousand-piece puzzle, knowing I'd stay with it until I snapped in the very last piece. Then she knew I'd let out a big, satisfied breath, take a few steps back, and see the whole picture.

Acknowledgments

Writing this book was one of the most challenging and rewarding experiences of my life. It opened my eyes wide and helped me uncover and make sense of many mysteries hidden in my past.

I'm filled with humility and gratitude when I think about all the people who helped me make this book happen. I owe my deepest gratitude to my loving husband of thirty-three years, Karl Schnakenburg, for his support from day one and for encouraging me to find my voice and never give up. To Kyle and Lexi, my children, who have been a positive force from the beginning and with grace and good humor pushed me to keep going, to think bigger.

I wish to thank my siblings, Roseann, Debbie, Robin, Barb, and Rob, for helping me finish this story, even as it meant collectively thrashing through some of the difficult times we endured as a family. I would like to thank my parents, survivors themselves, for their love and for being two of my most effective teachers.

I give thanks for the strength and generosity of Lee's children Pierre, Angel, and Serenity. Most of all, I thank God for being the silent whisper and the reason I kept coming back to the story, despite how difficult the excavation became. I now believe Lee's arrival at our doorstep in 1965 was a divine appointment of immeasurable love.

Finally, I thank Brooke Warner of She Writes Press for believing in this story and helping me bring it into the world.

I sincerely thank the editors and educators who helped me write this book and who made me a better writer.

Al Desette—book coach
Without your help, I might not even have left the starting gate.

Heather Demetrios—author, writing coach, meditation teacher
You not only helped me work through story ideas, you helped me stay centered while doing it.

Anne Helmstadter—author, writing structure coach
I thank you for helping me understand that a memoir isn't just a story but a story with beats.

Candi Cross—author, editor
You showed me how to focus. You taught me how to stay fired up when I really wanted to give up.

Curt Locklear—author, editor
Thanks to you for believing I could and would finish the story.

Lee Wade—author, writing teacher
I thank you for your encouragement and inspiration.

Cameron Dezen Hammon—author, writing educator, mentor
You taught me important things about writing, and you directed me to invaluable books on the craft.

Mary Rakow—author, editor
I thank you for helping me understand structure, a story's backbone.

David Colin Carr—author, editor
I'm grateful for your insights.

Michael Palgon—agent
I appreciate all our discussions that kept the story alive. Thank you for the inspiration.

Bernadette Murphy—editor
Thank you for your unending support.

And finally, **Jodi Fodor—writer, writing coach, editor**
For months you helped me rethink and revise the story, then you brought the sentences to life. You're the editor I just knew I was meant to partner with, and I'll never write another book without you.

I thank my Houston writing group:
Catherine Vance, Stefanie Fercking, Tanya Terry, Brooke Sum-mers-Perry, Robin Leonard, Mike Sheehan, Corin Bauman, and Nicole Moore-Kriel. Your suggestions and support were priceless!

And thank you to my beta readers:
Ann Dahn, Jennie Moran, Ava Ray, Susan Winkler, Karen Franz, Kelly Hull, and Marchel Peterson. Your detailed feed-back helped me improve the story.

These are only some of the writing books that have served as my teachers:

On Writing, Stephen King

Writing Down the Bones, Natalie Goldberg

Before and After the Book Deal, Courtney Maum

Atomic Habits, James Clear

The Writing Life, Julia Cameron and Natalie Goldberg

The Artist's Way, Julia Cameron

Storycraft, Jack Hart

Wired for Story, Lisa Cron

Story Genius, Lisa Cron

The War of Art, Steven Pressfield

Big Magic, Elizabeth Gilbert

The Power of Habit, Charles Duhigg

The Plot Whisperer, Martha Alderson

The Situation and the Story, Vivian Gornick

Invisible Ink, Brian McDonald

Steering the Craft, Ursula K. Le Guin

The Writer's Journey, Christopher Vogler

Plot & Structure, James Scott Bell

About the Author

Park City Photography

Sandra Schnakenburg grew up in Barrington, Illinois, and currently splits her time between Houston, Texas, and Park City, Utah. Early in her marriage, she and her husband lived in Melbourne, Australia, where they started a family. In 1999, after a decade overseas, they moved back to the United States to care for aging parents and spend more time with family. They raised their twins in The Woodlands, Texas.

After making a promise to Lee Metoyer on her deathbed, Sandra began researching and writing *The Housekeeper's Secret*. This is the story Lee asked her to write, and it is with honor and deep gratitude that she shares it with the world.

Sandra earned a BS in finance and international business from Arizona State University and an MBA specializing in finance and accounting from the University of Southern California. She left a career in corporate finance in 2010 and began to study creative nonfiction. She has completed writing courses at Writespace, Rice University, and The Writers University in Houston. *The Housekeeper's Secret* is her first book.

An excerpt of the story was published by The Write Launch in July 2022:
https://thewritelaunch.com/issues/
issue-sixty-three/2022/07/before-the-call/

Sandra's website: www.sandraschnakenburg.com.
Facebook: https://www.facebook.com/sandra.schnakenburg/
Instagram: https://www.instagram.com/sandrakschnakenburg/
Twitter: https://twitter.com/schnakenburgS

Looking for your next great read?

We can help!

Visit www.shewritespress.com/next-read
or scan the QR code below for a list
of our recommended titles.

She Writes Press is an award-winning
independent publishing company founded to
serve women writers everywhere.